Research Studies in Library Science, No. 3

RESEARCH STUDIES IN LIBRARY SCIENCE
Bohdan S. Wynar, Editor

No. 1. *Middle Class Attitudes and Public Library Use.* By Charles Evans; with an Introduction by Lawrence Allen.

No. 2. *Critical Guide to Catholic Reference Books.* By James Patrick McCabe, with an Introduction by Russell E. Bidlack.

No. 3. *An Analysis of Vocabulary Control in Library of Congress Classification and Subject Headings.* By John Phillip Immroth, with an Introduction by Jay E. Daily.

No. 4. *Research Methods in Library Science. A Bibliographic Guide.* By Bohdan S. Wynar.

No. 5. *Library Management: Behavior-Based Personnel Systems. A Framework for Analysis.* By Robert E. Kemper.

Analysis of Vocabulary Control in Library of Congress Classification and Subject Headings

---

JOHN PHILLIP IMMROTH

Introduction by
JAY E. DAILY
Professor of Library and Information Science
University of Pittsburgh

1971

LIBRARIES UNLIMITED, INC.   LITTLETON, COLORADO

TABLE OF CONTENTS

PREFACE 9

CHAPTER I.   INTRODUCTION 11
STATEMENT OF THE PROBLEM 11
THE NEED FOR THE STUDY 12
LIMITATIONS 15
TENTATIVE HYPOTHESES............................ 15

CHAPTER II.   PLAN FOR THE STUDY 18
LITERATURE SURVEY 18
   Indexes to Classification Schedules 19
   Subject Headings and Indexing 24
   Classified Catalog and Chain Indexing 31
   Conclusion 38
DATA COLLECTION METHODS 38
   Descriptive Analysis of the Individual L. C. Indexes 38
   Descriptive Analysis of the Relationship Between L. C. Subject
      Headings and L. C. Classification 39
   Experimental Models and Formulation of Rules for Chain
      Indexing 40
DEFINITION OF TERMS 42
   Descriptive Analysis of the Individual L. C. Indexes 42
   Descriptive Analysis of the Relationship Between L. C. Subject
      Headings and L. C. Classification 42
   Experimental Model and Formulation of Rules of Chain Indexing. 43

CHAPTER III.   DEVELOPMENT OF THE ARGUMENT FOR
             ANALYSIS OF L. C. INDEXES 49
ANALYSIS OF THE DATA COLLECTED 49
INTERPRETATION AND CONCLUSIONS 74

CHAPTER IV.   DEVELOPMENT OF THE ARGUMENT FOR
             ANALYSIS OF RELATIONSHIP BETWEEN L. C.
             SUBJECT HEADINGS AND L. C. CLASSIFICATION 83
INTRODUCTORY SUMMARY 83
ANALYSIS OF THE DATA COLLECTED 88
INTERPRETATIONS AND CONCLUSIONS 107

CHAPTER V. DEVELOPMENT OF THE ARGUMENT FOR
THE EXPERIMENTAL MODEL OF CHAIN
INDEXING L. C. CLASSIFICATION AND THE
FORMULATION OF RULES 109
INTRODUCTION 109
ANALYSIS OF DATA COLLECTED 117
INTERPRETATIONS AND CONCLUSIONS 128

CHAPTER VI. DEVELOPMENT OF THE ARGUMENT FOR
APPLICATION OF THE RULES TO ADDITIONAL
EXAMPLES 132
ANALYSIS OF THE DATA COLLECTED 132
INTERPRETATIONS AND CONCLUSIONS 135

CHAPTER VII. SUMMARY AND CONCLUSIONS 141
A SUMMARY OF THE ANALYSIS AND INTREPRETATION 141
THE DEFENSE OF THE HYPOTHESIS 142
THE IMPLICATIONS OF THIS STUDY 143
THE CONCLUSION 144
SUGGESTIONS FOR FURTHER RESEARCH 145

CHAPTER VIII. LIST OF WORKS CONSULTED 147

APPENDIX 156
SHAKESPEARE CHAIN INDEX—ALPHABETICAL ARRAY 156
SHAKESPEARE FEATURE CARDS—CLASSIFIED ARRAY 171

ACKNOWLEDGMENTS

The author wishes to acknowledge the encouragement, advice, inspiration and enthusiasm given to him by his major advisor Dr. Jay E. Daily, Professor of Library and Information Sciences, University of Pittsburgh. I am also indebted to the other members of my dissertation committee: Prof. Allen Kent, Director of Communications; Dr. Frank B. Sessa, Professor of Library and Information Science; Dr. Casimir Borkowski, Associate Professor of Library and Information Science; and Dr. Rae Siporin, Asst. Dean of Arts and Science, University of Pittsburgh. Further I am indebted to Mrs. Darlene Fawcett for the typing of the original manuscript including the many lengthy supplementary tables and appendices. Finally, I wish to thank my wife, Barbara, for her continuing patience, assistance and encouragement.

Pittsburgh, September 23, 1970   J.P.I.

PREFACE

Doctoral dissertations have, at times justifiedly, earned a poor reputation among the intellectual products of Academe. The best, and it is my pleasure to write about the best here, give the impression that the work would have done even if Academe's highest honor were not the reward sought. An earned doctorate represents a fearful amount of work which only one who has run the course (or braved the gauntlet) can understand. At some point in the student's work he feels a hopelessness and despair that can hardly be described but is instantly recognized by anyone who has endured the feeling. He stands beyond all help, at the furthest edge of present knowledge, in the dark and alone. His advisor can not offer solutions, even if he knows them, lest the chief advantage of the effort be lost. The student must have the opportunity of discovering for himself what will advance knowledge.

He is fortunate indeed if he can settle a major, or even a minor, point of contention among scholars, and doubly fortunate if his effort improves the practices and understanding in his profession. The student comes to think of his advisor, if their relation has been a happy one, as something of a father or at least a kindly uncle, and the advisor thinks of his student as an Oriental paterfamilias regards his adult son who has sired a son of his own. There is a continuance, almost a family tree of dissertations, and Dr. Immroth's work represents the second generation in studies which began under Professor Maurice Tauber at Columbia University. The blood-lines, though attenuated, are still there, and something of Professor Tauber's practicality, his intense love and understanding of the scientific method, is better represented in Dr. Immroth's work than in my own.

It is customary for a student to thank his advisor, but it is a rare privilege for the advisor to be able to thank his student. Aside from giving his advisor a better reputation than he deserves, Dr. Immroth's dissertation advances work in an area which has been characterized by much opinion and few validated conclusions. It was timely to the point that word was rushed to the Library of Congress advising against any project that would have combined in one alphabet the indexes of the several schedules. Dr. Immroth shows why this would be a major labor with results far less than the cost would justify. The portion of a basic course in cataloging which advised students that the Subject Headings Used in the Dictionary Catalogs of the Library of Congress could be used as an index to the Library of Congress classification was quickly negated, and another dissertation in progress was radically altered because of the results of Dr. Immroth's work. For all these swiftly realized benefits, I am deeply grateful.

But I am more grateful for the future of subject analysis which Dr. Immroth's work at last clarifies. That the chain index will remain as the most efficient method of subject analysis is all the more a reliable prediction because of Dr. Immroth's destruction of any necessary ligature between the notation of a classification and its natural language schedules. It was brave indeed to challenge the accepted view that the Library of Congress classification could not be used for chain indexing. It is apparent that it can, and it must, if great research libraries are to provide the subject access to their collections that the abundance of information sources demands. Hence we can look forward to a time when the hit-or-miss methods of subject analysis so far used by the Library of Congress, and all other libraries which depend upon it for this vital service to patrons, will be supplanted by the controlled methods that Dr. Immroth's work make possible. We can see a time when the rigidity of the catalog will not determine the accessibility of information, but rather the conclusiveness of the rules will at once liberate subject analysis from unnecessary constraint and preserve its practice from the caprice of the individual cataloger.

In a sense, Dr. Immroth has prepared that first document from which all others will grow. He has not written a cookbook for chain indexers, he has set methods and standards for all future cookbooks, an accomplishment rather like those discoveries which led to aseptic surgery or to self-propelled vehicles. Granted that the discovery is world-shaking only to the fully informed in the general area of subject analysis, it is nonetheless important and its full importance will be understood when the succeeding years have shown that without Dr. Immroth's work, we would have no hope for the improvement of our subject catalogs. Now only the effort necessary to follow the directions laid down prevents the renewal of our collections by the marvelous method of making them far more usable than before. Just how important this is can best be illustrated by reminding the reader that the development of genetics was delayed for more than a generation because Mendel's work lay hidden in the great libraries of the world, unknown for want of sufficient access to the information contained in the obscure Prussian periodical which published the essays of an even more obscure priest.

The University of Pittsburgh has no means of honoring its most distinguished doctoral candidates beyond the degree and very likely it needs none. The reward is chiefly in the work done, in its permanence and influence, and ultimately in finding one's own effort improved upon by a brilliant student. My only wish for Dr. Immroth is that he can direct a dissertation with as much pleasure and satisfaction as I have enjoyed, and thus continue an investigation that began with a study of reclassification and continued with an analysis of subject headings and has led to the methodology of subject analysis for the greatest classification extant here available with precision and clarity sooner than anyone could have hoped for two years ago.

JAY E. DAILY
Professor of Library and Information Science

Pittsburgh, September 4, 1970

CHAPTER I

INTRODUCTION

STATEMENT OF THE PROBLEM

The process of subject cataloging at the Library of Congress is concerned with the assignment of classification numbers and subject headings in accordance with the Library's classification schedules and the Library's List of Subject Headings. Inherent in the use of these schedules and lists is the language used as descriptors or subject headings whether in classified or alphabetical order. Each specific subject may have two or even three different descriptors as a result. There is the vocabulary of the classification schedules, the vocabulary of the subject headings, and in some cases the vocabulary of the indexes to the classification schedules.

The existence of these different vocabularies or subsets of language in the process of subject cataloging at the Library of Congress is the basic problem to be investigated in this study. Classification and subject headings may be said to provide the basic subject access to a library's holdings. As Jack Mills states, "A library which fails to make its own index to the systematic arrangement of its stock is failing in its service to its readers and in its use of a valuable tool."[1] It may be further observed, as Allen Kent does, that indexing and subject cataloging are synonymous.[2] In addition the actual processes of assigning classification numbers and subject headings are basically the same intellectual process as stated by E. J. Coates, "The two disciplines only diverge at the subsequent phase in which the abstracted idea is reformulated by the subject cataloguer as a subject heading and by the classifier as a classification symbol."[3] Leonard Jolley discerns that the actual development of a list of subject headings is an act of classification.[4] As a direct result of the identity of the processes of classification and subject headings both Jay E. Daily and Jean Perreault have asked why the vocabularies are not the same:

> Would it be possible to make the entries in the relative index
> to a classification and the subject headings the same?[5]
> Why are not subject-headings and classification organized
> into one rather than two system(s)?[6]

This study investigates descriptively first, the relationship between the classification schedules and their indexes and second, the relationship between subject headings and the classification headings. The third phase of this study develops an experimental model of a chain index which may serve as both an

11

index to the classification and a list of subject headings. As this model is developed all necessary rules for chain indexing of L. C. classification will be formulated. These rules will then be applied to additional parts of the classification.

THE NEED FOR THE STUDY

Generally students are taught to classify materials directly from the classification tables and not from the indexes.[7] In fact, one of the foremost twentieth century scholars and teachers of classification, the late W. C. Berwick Sayers, recommends only using the index as a "mere check" after consulting the tables.[8] Classifiers usually become so familiar with the main tables that they do not use the index except with "great caution" as the historian of American classification, Leo LaMontagne, states.[9] British librarian T. MacCallum Walker states further,

> Teachers of classification have always advocated (probably
> rightly) that the classifier should work directly from the
> schedules, using the index only as a check. The consequence
> has been that attention has been deflected from the index
> to the schedules and it is mainly on these that the merits
> of a classification scheme are judged. Only now, when the
> advent of chain indexing procedures focuses more attention
> on the subject index and only when the index itself is made
> fully relative, will it be appreciated how much in advance of
> his time was Dewey.[10]

It may be observed further that some of the Library of Congress schedules have no index, [11] and yet are regularly and effectively used. In addition there is no general index to L. C. classification. There are, of course, at least three possible partial substitutions for a general index.[12] These are the list of L. C. Subject Headings, the *Index to the Classed Catalog of the Boston University Libraries*, and the *Subject and Name Index of Books* of the Edinburgh Public Library.

Sayers states in his canons and criteria of classification that a classification system needs to have "An index which shall provide a means of rapid reference to the place of any term in the schedules of the scheme."[13] He writes in regard specifically to the L. C. indexes, "It is scarcely possible to imagine an index carried to greater fulness."[14] A similar view is presented by Margaret Mann.

> The indexes are very full, including geographical entries,
> personal names when used as subjects, names of battles,
> and other topics frequently omitted from such lists. Refer-
> ences are made from different forms of names and attention
> is sometimes directed to related subjects.[15]

12

La Montagne, however, points out that the individual indexes are of "varying fullness"[16] and modern British classificationist, Jack Mills, discerns that some indexes "fail to show the 'distributed relatives' as clearly as a good relative index should" and that there are "often surprising omissions."[17] The wide variation of these comments seems to justify not only the need to discern the internal function of these indexes but also to attempt to determine the logical development of these indexes. This may be of further importance if the proposed cumulation of all these indexes into a general index is attempted. In fact the question may be posed: can these separate indexes be simply interfiled to generate a general index. In 1961, LaMontagne stated,

> One of the most frequent, non-theoretical criticisms of the
> L. C. Classification is that it has no general, or combined,
> Index. A start toward the compilation of one was made in
> 1947, when all existing indexes were cut and mounted on
> cards. Although lack of funds prevented the cutting of sub-
> entries, the mounted cards fill 60 trays. Excluding Law
> index entries, which will not be available for some time, a
> combined index would constitute a volume of approximately
> 1,000 pages containing 100,000 entries. In view of the
> present workload no date of publication can be given.[18]

Sayers refers to this proposed general index as "an instrument of great value"[19] and Richard S. Angell, of the staff of the Library of Congress, implies that a general index will be completed after the compilation of Class K: Law.[20] In May of 1967, the first subclass KF, Law of the United States, was issued.[21] Another reason for the justification of this study would be to ascertain if these individual indexes could be used to form an index to a classified catalog using chain indexes.

Further, the question of whether or not the index to a classification schedule could be used as a list of subject headings was raised in a speech given by Jay E. Daily in 1957.

> Would it be possible to make the entries in the relative
> index to a classification and the subject headings the same?
> The traditions of catalogers have been quite different. There
> is now no complete code of practice which will make clear
> to subject catalogers what Merrills' Code does for classifiers
> of books. Perhaps, since both classification and subject
> cataloging are usually done by the same person, we need
> one for both.

> Let us assume that we try to devise a method that would
> enable us to discover whether there is a possibility of
> constructing a classification the relative index of which
> would be a list of subject headings. We must first discover
> what point of similarity there is between classification and

lists of subject headings. The answer, it seems to me, is that both deal with language in its broadest, general sense. A list of subject headings is a special use of vernacular language. A classification employs a highly specialized language—notation— and, in the schedules, provides it with a translation, which also shows the grammar of the notation.[22]

Such an arrangement would allow a genuine sense of subject integrity to be present. If a subject heading list were truly an index to a related subject classification, then one could assume that the terms in the index came from the classification schedule; or, that the classification schedule itself was a list of classified subject headings or descriptors; or, that the list of subject headings was simply the classification headings arranged in an alphabetical array. The classified approach to a list of subject headings or descriptors, such as does exist in various forms of category lists and hierarchical trees, could be extended to a related classification scheme by this arrangement.

One of the reasons for the need for this study is to estimate how close the L. C. subject headings and L. C. classification come to this reversible concept. Normally it seems that separate forms of vocabulary control are applied to alphabetical subject indexes and to headings in a classification schedule. A heading in a classification schedule may use fewer words because of the context of other headings than an isolated heading in a simple alphabetical array.[23] Another parameter is the transformation of the classification heading from its classified form, to its form in the index to the classification scheme. The vocabulary control which is used on lists of subject headings usually involves the "translation from natural (source) language to 'key word' (index entries for purpose of facilitating alphabetization of a subject index)."[24]

If a positive relationship of terminology may be discerned in this study, the beginnings of a code for subject analysis may be made. Even a negative relationship would be useful for understanding the differences in the application of subject analysis. In either case there are obvious further implications for study in this area: 1) the relationship of an index to a classified catalog to both areas of subject cataloging and, 2) the possibilities of chain indexing if developed in relation to integrated terminology of chain index, classification schedule, classification index, and subject headings.

As a direct result of these implications the author feels justified in studying the possibilities of chain indexing of L. C. classification. Such a model will have to follow strict structural and semantic rules to integrate the vocabulary of the chain index, the classification schedule, the classification index, and the subject headings. This model could then allow the chain index to be the subject headings. Further this model would allow the classification schedules to be fully indexed. This constructive approach resulting from the third phase of this study generates a vocabulary for subject analysis. The use of this vocabulary control would not be limited to Library of Congress subject cataloging but could have implications for all classification schemes, subject heading lists, and perhaps most important, specialized information science thesauri.

LIMITATIONS

As systems of both classification and subject headings have been developed by the Library of Congress, and as these headings represent the largest body of vocabulary of any subject analysis system in English, it seems appropriate and fitting to use these two systems as the universe of discourse for this study. The limitations are the analysis of portions of the vocabulary of the Library of Congress classification schedules, their indexes, and the Library of Congress *List of Subject Headings*. This study will not be concerned with either of the two published external indexes (Boston and Edinburgh[25]) or the empirical applications of subject analysis at the Library of Congress. As a result of these limitations the following tentative hypotheses may be stated.

TENTATIVE HYPOTHESES

The first hypothesis of this study is that the indexes for individual Library of Congress classification schedules vary in fullness and do not represent a single logical development.

The second tentative hypothesis of this study is that there is a discernible relationship, demonstrating a high percentage of identity, between the terminology of the L. C. subject headings and the L. C. classification.

The third tentative hypothesis is that the use of chain indexing will unify the vocabulary of the Library's subject cataloging so that an alphabetical array of the classification will be a list of subject headings and that a classified array of subject headings will be the classification schedule.

[1] Jack Mills, "Chain Indexing and the Classified Catalogue," *Library Association Record*, LVII (April, 1955), 143.

[2] Allen Kent, *Textbook on Mechanized Information Retrieval*, Library Science and Documentation, A Series of Texts and Monographs, Vol. III (2d ed.; New York: Interscience Publishers, 1966), p. 113.

[3] E. J. Coates, *Subject Catalogues, Headings and Structure* (London: Library Association, 1960), p. 16.

[4] Leonard Jolley, *The Principles of Cataloguing*, with a foreword by R. O. MacKenna (New York: Philosophical Library, 1960), p. 104.

[5] Jay E. Daily, "Subject Headings and the Theory of Classification," *American Documentation*, VII (October, 1957), 270

[6] Jean M. Perreault, "On Bibliography and Automation: or, How to Reinvent the Catalog," *Libri*, XV (1965), 309.

[7] W. C. Berwick Sayers, *A Manual of Classification for Librarians and Bibliographers* (3d ed. rev.; London: Andre Deutsch, 1959), p. 78; Margaret Mann, *Introduction to Cataloging and the Classification of Books* (2d ed.; Chicago; American Library Association, 1943), p. 54; Bohdan S. Wynar, *Introduction to Cataloging and Classification*, Library Science Text Series (3d ed.; Littleton, Colo.: Libraries Unlimited, 1967), p. 194.

[8] Sayers, *loc. cit.*

[9] Leo E. LaMontagne, *American Library Classification with Special Reference to the Library of Congress* (Hamden, Conn.: Shoe String Press, 1961), p. 22.

[10] T. MacCallum Walker, "The Subject-Approach in the University Library," *Libri*, VI (1956), 264-65.

[11] John Phillip Immroth, *A Guide to Library of Congress Classification*, Rochester, N.Y.: Libraries Unlimited, 1968), p. 33.

[12] *Ibid.*, pp. 84-85.

[13] Sayers, *op. cit.*, p. 81.

[14] *Ibid.*, p. 170.

[15] Mann, *op. cit.*, p. 82.

[16] LaMontagne, *op. cit.*, p. 213.

[17] Jack Mills, *A Modern Outline of Library Classification* (London: Chapman and Hall, 1960), pp. 98-99.

[18] LaMontagne, *op. cit.*, p. 339.

[19] Sayers, *op. cit.*, p. 169.

[20] Richard S. Angell, "Development of Class K at the Library of Congress," *Law Library Journal*, LVII (November, 1964), 335.

[21] Immroth, *op. cit.*, pp. 222-225.

[22] Daily, *loc. cit.*

[23] Kent, *op. cit.*, p. 238.

[24] *Idem.*

[25] *Supra,* p. 12, fn. 12.

CHAPTER II

PLAN FOR THE STUDY

LITERATURE SURVEY

All general and specialized works, articles and chapters of books dealing with L. C. classification have been surveyed beginning with the bibliographies in *A Guide to Library of Congress Classification.*[1] In addition works dealing with indexing, subject headings, subject analysis, classified catalogs and chain indexing have been searched. These concomitant areas all suggest approaches for further study and seem to validate this investigation. Although the literature survey of material on L. C. classification yielded little result, the other areas proved to be most fruitful. As the previous chapter contains the most pertinent results of the L. C. classification literature survey, this section will deal mainly with these other areas: 1) indexes to classification systems, 2) subject headings in relation to alphabetical subject catalogs and indexes, and 3) the classified catalog and its index.

As already discussed in the first chapter, difficulties in integrating classification and subject headings arise from the traditional separation of these two activities in the cataloging department. Traditionally classification has been the responsibility fo the classifier or perhaps subject cataloger, while subject headings have been assigned by the descriptive cataloger. Cataloging departments are often partitioned in this fashion as are introductory textbooks. This may be seen in the following quotation from James Duff Brown writing in a British examination guidebook in 1916.

> A classifier makes up his mind what is the dominant subject
> matter of the book, and where it is likely to be most
> required, and places it at that appropriate class. The
> cataloger, on the other hand, need not trouble himself as
> to the chief topic handled, because he deals with entries,
> not with books, and can classify and index a work under
> as many headings as he deems necessary. His function is
> to provide descriptions of books so that they arrange in a
> definite order, and the inquirer is enabled to find the
> literature of all aspects of a subject assembled at get-at-able
> places. The 'relative' indexes to certain systems of classifi-
> cation are of greater assistance to a cataloguer than to a
> classifier, because they suggest alternative headings, and to
> some extent point out the aspects and standpoints of a
> subject.[2]

The last sentence of the above quotation shows an interesting relationship between subject headings and the indexes to classification schemes which will be pursued in the following section of this chapter. Obviously the traditional approach of separating classification and subject heading work is not economic so far as subject analysis is concerned. Richard Angell in a seminar panel discussion of John Metcalfe's paper on the alphabetical subject indication of information discerns the close relationship of classification and subject headings. He states that subject headings lists should not be tied to classification, generally or in a particular system, but that "there should be a hierarchical base in making downward references to a new heading, and that a classificatory tree was in their minds at the Library of Congress and should be in the minds of those making subject heading lists."[3] The possibility that a classification and a subject heading list might be identical is called a "remarkable conclusion"[4] by Frederick Jonker in 1964. However, classification and subject cataloging should be a single operation according to E. J. Coates.

> The operation here called summarisation, the abstraction of the overall idea embodied in the subject content of a given literary unit, besides being basic to most forms of subject cataloguing, is also the most important process in subject classification. "The two disciplines only diverge at the subsequent phase in which the abstracted idea is reformulated by the subject cataloguer as a subject heading and by the classifier as a classification symbol." Both techniques provide answers to the question "what is the subject of this document?" which are different in form alone.[5]

In order to examine the ideas presented in this introductory section in more depth, this writer shall attempt to investigate the integration of classification and subject headings in each of the following sections.

Indexes to Classification Schedules

One of the foremost twentieth century scholars and teachers of classification, the late W. C. Berwick Sayers, states in his canons and criteria of classification for books that a classification system needs to have "An index which shall provide a means of rapid reference to the place of any term in the schedules of the scheme."[6] A modern British classificationist, Jack Mills, discusses two functions for an alphabetical subject index: first, "to act as a key to the location of topics" and second, "to provide a supplementary classification, by bringing together all those aspects and relations of a topic which are not brought together in the systematic arrangement."[7] Perhaps, a more complete definition is given by another British classificationist, B. C. Vickery.

> A subject index consists, in the first place, of an assembly of references to items of information. Each reference is labelled—

by a number, by letters, by words, by what we call in general a *heading*—and the headings must be related in the mind of the searcher to the subject he seeks, and so constructed or so arranged that any particular heading can be located.

An index must set out to do more than this, because the references sought, although in the index, may not bear the heading which the searcher tries to locate. There are several reasons for this. The searcher may not name his specific subject exactly; he may name a broader, narrower or allied subject, and so will look for the wrong heading; the index may record references to studies on broader, narrower or allied subjects which have a bearing on the subject sought, but these will not be revealed by the references actually located. The index must therefore be more than an orderly arrangement of labelled references: it must also reveal the relations existing between the headings, i.e., the relations existing in the subject matter indexed.[8]

This definition of an index closely fits the concept of Sayers in regard to a relative index. He discerns two kinds of indexes: a specific index in which a subject may be listed in only one place and a relative index "which gives the one entry, but adds to it all the views, standpoints, and relationships, as well as synonymous words, in fact, everything that may form a sub-section of the subject indexed."[9] Australian Library educator, John Metcalfe, finds the relative index to be simply an index to the classification "to its subjects in their different class relations."[10] Melvil Dewey writing in his own particular form of simplified spelling says of his own relative index, "The index gives similar or sinonimus words, and the same words in different connections, so any intelijent person wil surely get the ryt number [sic] ."[11] Benjamin Custer writes of the current edition of the Dewey Decimal Classification,

> 3.61 The index is *relative* (and is traditionally known as the "relative index"): rather than recapitulate the tables alphabetically, it reverses them, in that it brings together the various aspects of a subject to show their dispersion thruout the tables. For example, if you have a book on botanical drugs and look under that term, you will find several aspects and subaspects, including chemistry, general pharmacology, and veterinary pharmacology, each leading you to a number in the tables.[12]

Mills discusses the distinction made between a specific index and a relative one.

> The relative index gives against each term class numbers for all the different aspects of the topic which are in the

classification. The 'specific index', a name given by Sayers to the index of the SC, gives only the one entry per term, e.g., *Petroleum D813; Economics L100.* But whereas the first entry is perfectly accurate (everything on Petroleum really is at D813) the second is thoroughly misleading, since L100 takes only the Problem and Place facets of Economics—the economics of particular industries are subordinated to the industries. So a 'specific' index is not really a different kind of index to a systematic sequence—only an undeveloped one.[13]

Further he states in another source, "Dewey's Relative Index has always shown an awareness of the economies possible, giving class numbers in heavy type when they are further divided in the classification. But it has many inconsistencies."[14] The opposite point of view may be found in the following quotation from the developer of the *Subject Classification* and hence of the idea of a specific, not a relative index. James Duff Brown states,

> But, perhaps, the least satisfactory feature of the Decimal classification, apart from its somewhat illogical basis, is the provision of a rather superficial and selective "Relative Index," which at one time was hailed as a very important and valuable accessor. Time has considerably modified that view, and it is being gradually recognized that a scheme of classification should confine itself to the relative placing of topics, leaving standpoints to be determined by cataloguers. A relative index is supposed to give all kinds of associations, categories, styles of treatment, and phases which may qualify subjects, and its object is to suggest to the user possible alternative places for every subject. This means that practically every subject could be qualified by hundreds of other subjects or phases, and thus it is evident that instead of assisting a classifier, it can only end in confusing and hindering. It is not the part of an index to a system of classification to do more than direct the classifier to the place in a schedule where a subject number is to be found, after he has determined what that subject is. One of the series of 'Canons' for judging of the completeness of a classification, drawn up by Mr. W. D. B. Sayers, lays it down as a law that 'It must be furnished with a relative index; that is to say, an index showing the place of every topic, and every phase or view of a topic.' A very little reflection will show that such an index, while useful for the cataloguer, would only embarrass the classifier by its size and complexity. If every subject is to be analysed, and its qualifying categories added in a complete manner, and not in the partial and selective style of the 'Decimal' index, the result is going to be rather appalling.[15]

It may be that Mills' concept of an undeveloped relative index is true of both Brown's *Subject Classification* and Dewey's *Decimal Classification*. Custer points out that the index to the present edition is limited: "only those aspects appearing most frequently in the literature are included"; and "still another form of limitation is the deliverate omission of thousands of terms, obviously parts of broader concepts, the inclusion of which would make the index look more like an unabridged dictionary."[16]

From the preceding discussion and presentations of definitions it may be discerned that the term relative index has many different meanings. It appears that a relative index may be very relative at times but not at other times as is particularly the case with most editions of the *Dewey Decimal Classification*. Perhaps the most relative index or at all events the best relative index would result from chain indexing. It also would appear that a relative index may tend to avoid vocabulary control or at least not find vocabulary control as important an operation as it would be in a straight alphabetic subject index. Brown's attitude toward a relative index is just as interesting today as it was in 1916.

> It was the lack of proper alphabetical indexes in classified catalogues and schemes which caused DeMorgan, Jevons, and other writers to decry subject classification and classed catalogues. The misconceptions of the past and the necessities of the present point therefore to a full alphabetical (non-relative) index as an indispensable adjunct to every classification scheme or systemically classified catalogue.[17]

Coates sees the direct relation of the relative index to the chain index.

> In any alphabetical subject index to a classification, some related subject separated in the classification will be brought together through verbal similarities. This occurs in a some-what haphazard and arbitrary fashion because single words stand for complex ideas. If all ideas could be represented in the index only by means of combinations of elementary constituent terms, collation in index sequence would signal relationships comprehensively. Chain procedure indexing, reflecting the modulated structure of the classification scheme, tends to represent complex ideas by means of elementary combined terms, rather than by single complex terms: because of this, the coverage of subject relationship signalled by a classified catalogue supported by collation of terms in the chain procedure index is probably greater than that produced by any alternative method of indexing.[18]

It is interesting to observe that Ranganathan's *Colon Classification* uses a chain index to index its schedules.[19]

As it has already been noted in chapter one, L. C. classification does not have a unified relative, specific or chain index.[20] Mary Herrick in an article on the development of the classified catalog at Boston University comments,

The absence of a relative index to the LC has always made
its application more difficult. Only within the last few years
has there been any indication that the LC is working toward
one. This is so recent and additions are so few in the
Topical indexes, they offer little help at present. The
subject heading list and the brief topical indexes at the
ends of the separate schedules continue to be the bases
of all major approaches to the schedule. It was, therefore,
necessary to set up our own index, and in the first two
years or so, the LC subject heading list was of considerable
help.[21]

This use of subject headings as index terms in a classified catalog will be
discussed in a following section of this survey. Another similar idea is suggested
by Desmond Taylor. "Also, the *Books: Subjects* catalogs, like the LC *Subject
Headings*, can function as a very effective index to Library of Congress schedules."[22] Directly related to these two comments is Phyllis Richmond's concept
of a unified L. C. index.

These indexes are satisfactory to use because they have so
many synonymous terms. A unified index to the whole
probably would add to this feature. Also, when made, a
unified index could be matched with the LC list of subject
headings, strengthening what is now a loose connection
between the two. One of the advantages of using the subject-
headings list is that LC class numbers are given with a great
many subject headings, offering a lead into the classification
for the perplexed. It is not so good a lead as through the
subject catalog for seeking precedents, but sometimes all
one needs is a hint, not a thorough survey. With the
seventh edition of the subject headings in machine-
readable form, putting the index to the classification in
similar form and matching the two might make each a
better tool than it is at present.[23]

The diversity of opinion between Richmond and Herrick should be pointed
out. While Richmond finds the individual indexes to be satisfactory, Herrick
finds them offering little help. If these two comments are considered in the
light of the previous differences of opinion concerning the indexes as shown
in chapter one, the first hypothesis of this study appears to be worthy of
objective study. Further there appears to be nothing in all these comments
on classification indexes which would seriously preclude the possibility of
the terms in an index to a classification schedule from being subject headings.
The relativity of the index seems mainly to determine the order not the type
of term in the index.

Subject Headings and Indexing

Subject access in the traditional dictionary catalog or a separate alphabetical subject catalog is provided by means of individual subject descriptors or subject headings. These descriptors or headings usually are selected from established authority files, printed thesauri or subject heading lists. The assignment of a subject heading or a descriptor or an index term may be considered as virtually the same process of subject analysis. Jonker defines indexing as "the art of assigning one or more terms to an 'item of information' so as to characterize it. The word 'term' is used here in its broadest sense and comprises any form of class, subclass, subject heading, single word or combination of words."[24] Allen Kent discerns that indexing and subject cataloging are very similar operations.

> It will be evident that from many points of view, the terms 'indexing' and 'subject cataloging' are synonymous. The principles of analysis required to conduct cataloging and indexing appear to be identical—certainly with regard to basic objectives.[25]

One of these lists of descriptors, *The List of Subject Headings Used in the Dictionary Catalogs of the Library of Congress*, is directly related to this study.

Subject headings in general and L. C. subject headings in particular have been the topic of much criticism and debate. George Scheerer in 1957 writes,

> Neither the catchword subject catalog nor the alphabetical classed catalog has been given a fair trial; both were rejected. But the second "parent" of the dictionary catalog, the classed catalog, when transposed into alphabetical arrangement, becomes the alphabetical classed catalog. It is not surprising, therefore, that the dictionary subject catalog is a compromise between the two. The embodiment of the compromise is the impressionistic subject heading list: an alphabetical arrangement of catchwords ("specific" entries) tied together, consciously or unconsciously, but the use of classification features.[26]

The concept of the inherent classificatory features of subject headings will be discussed in a later part of this section. It should be noted at this point however that the relationships of language and vocabulary control to classification is most important.

The value of using subject headings or subject catalogs is open to question. Leonard Jolley discerns this attitude in his *Principles of Cataloguing*.

> Some librarians have claimed that a subject catalogue is not needed in a learned library. The student is directed to books

by his teachers and the more advanced worker finds his subject approach to books from bibliographies and from references in the literature itself.[27]

And Scheerer bluntly states, "The inadequate subject index of the dictionary catalog is turning users away from it when their purpose is serious research."[28] Defense of subject headings may be found in the writings of Julia Pettee[29] David Haykin[30], and Oliver Lilley[31] among others.

Perhaps one of the major problems with subject headings and their control is involved with Cutter's concept of specific entry. This idea is found in rule 161: "Enter a work under its subject-heading, not under a class which includes that subject."[32] Mills writes of this,

> Theoretically, entry is *specific* (i.e., not under a more general subject heading) and *direct* (i.e., it reflects the form ordinary usage would suggest—that which the reader would first use when looking for the subject, rather than inverted forms, or a statement of general class and subdivision, such as *Architecture—Houses—Georgian*.)
>
> In practice, specific entry is often—even usually—shunned, even in such elaborate lists of subject headings as those of the Library of Congress.[33]

Harry Dewey blames the problem of works dealing with multiple subjects on the lack of specific entry.

> Incidentally, it is LC's failure to employ specific entry that is responsible for the impression, widely held among librarians, that books often deal with two subjects. Only a few do so. Examine a hundred LC cards with two subject headings and you will find that most of them actually deal with a single topic.[34]

Perreault discerns that a work deals with a single subject not with multiple subjects. Only the lack of precise headings force us to use several headings for one concept.

> Documents are on *one* subject, but that subject is likely to be a complex of several elements each of which may be a subject by itself, or may be an element in an otherwise wholly different complex subject; authors are not predictable, on the basis of past history, as to the new complexes their works may occasion. What therefore is needed is an information language that is flexible not in allowing alternative locations, but in allowing unforeseen complexes to arise as needed, to keep up with the troublesome unpredictability of authors.[35]

Directly related to this problem of specific or generic term is the use of subdivision of a subject heading. Paul Dunkin points out,

> So Cutter allowed subject heading subdivision; but he tried
> to allow it only to make the entries under a subject heading
> easier for the user to find.

> One question remained: If the original subject heading could
> be subdivided in *any*way, was it *truly* the direct and specific
> subject heading for the books listed under it?[36]

Another common criticism of L. C. subject headings is the syndetic structure. In this vein Perreault states,

> But first it is necessary to remember that the see-also
> references in LC subject-headings (and in Sears as well,
> of course, based as it is upon LC) are not thoroughly
> organized to provide chains from broadest to narrowest,
> especially when the terms are proper names. Nor are LC
> "see-also" references unambiguous; they indiscriminately
> refer to subordinates, coordinates, correlates, and even
> occasionally to superordinates.[37]

A further problem is the actual assignment of these headings by the cataloger. Scheerer repeats a typical criticism of this assignment. "To this day, as some LC cards demonstrate, catalogers use the leading words of the title as the key to the subject heading, sometimes overlooking the real subject of the book completely."[38] Perhaps the practical situation may be simply summed up as Daily does, "As it is at present, there is no part of cataloging which is more guess-work and more frustrating. There is simply no way but prejudice and preconception to determine which is the better subject heading and why."[39] Dunkin answers the obvious question of why writers attempt to defend subject headings.

> Moreover, the published list freezes practice, particularly
> if the list's headings appear on printed cards such as those
> of LC or Wilson. Over the years these cards build up in
> the library a big investment in the status quo of subject
> heading work. It would be costly to change basic philos-
> ophy; it is much easier to rationalize practice, as Haykin
> and Julia Pettee did.[40]

Another of the basic problems with subject headings and their vocabulary control is a linguistic problem. Farradane writes,

> Language is not an accurate tool; it has evolved, in all its
> varieties and nuances, mainly for the purpose of daily
> living, without the need for accuracy, with a multiplicity
> of local connotations and usages, and is mostly highly

26

charged emotionally, so that facial or manual gestures are added to supplement meaning. It is one of the important tasks of science, in the presentation of accurate knowledge, to give single, unambiguous definitions to words, or to invent a 'jargon' of new words where the old will not do. This is easiest with nouns or verbal nouns and some verbs, and few attempts have been made with other parts of speech.[41]

Coates points out the importance of language to classification.

Research in classification is making an attempt to forge an instrument of communication without the crudities of natural language; but we should not overlook the fact that natural language is the soil out of which classification has grown. In the future development of classification it would be most unwise to disregard the hints and intimations which ordinary language offers on concept relationships. Neither in its theory nor in its practice can classification detach itself completely from its affiliations with language.[42]

The basic problem appears to be as Farradane states, "We cannot classify 'things' themselves, but only our concepts representative of the 'things'. This is no quibble, and we must constantly bear in mind how we obtain our concepts and how we interrelate them in our minds."[43] The linguistic basis of vocabulary control in both subject headings and classification headings is noted by Perreault, ". . . a systematic conceptual organization is an artificial *language*, and must therefore have both a vocabulary and a *syntax*."[44] Vickery presents some elementary rules for vocabulary control that are applicable to either indexing or subject headings.

In controlling the vocabulary of an alphabetical index, the first step is to restrict the number of types of heading used. As shown in Chapter I, Marie Prevost urged the use of noun combinations whenever possible. Prepositional phrases can usually be replaced by a noun combination (e.g., Fertilization of flowers by Flowers—Fertilization), but some have to be retained since the phrase as a whole has a specialized meaning (e.g., Bodies of revolution). Adjectival phrases cannot be avoided so readily, as they are needed to specify entities which have no individual name (e.g., Actino-mycete antibiotics). Nevertheless, the target at which to aim is a co-ordinated succession of nouns, qualified nouns (adjectival phrases) or prepositional phrases acting as nouns.[45]

If one turns directly to rules for the control of vocabulary in the development of subject headings, there are several possible codes or approaches. One of the most important for library science is the approach of Charles Ammi

Cutter in his *Rules for a Dictionary Catalog.* There are eighteen specific rules presented for the formation of subject headings.[46] These rules are the basis for the current list of subject headings issued by the Library of Congress. The value and precision of these rules are open to question. Jay E. Daily in his *Grammar of Subject Headings* seriously questions Cutter's rules and presents some fifteen rules of his own.[47] John Metcalfe attempts to bring Cutter's rules up-to-date with "Tentative Code of Rules for Alphabetico-specific Entry."[48] Besides Daily's and Metcalfe's work with Cutter's rules, other writers have attacked Cutter. Marie Prevost writes,

> Cutter was set, once for all, on the haphazard adjective approach to subjects; and all of us became set with him and thereby committed to a series of rules most of which contain provisions for their own reversal. The clear wisdom of Schwartz was swept into the discard; and slowly the subject currents in our dictionary catalogs have multiplied and collided until we do not know where we are going at any moment.[49]

And Scheerer again with characteristic bluntness states, "This is 1957, and it is time to bury Cutter."[50] Other possible rules for vocabulary control include the work of Otto Kaiser, Julia Pettee, Marie Prevost, Mortimer Taube, A. Thompson, etc. In fact one may turn to almost any system for information retrieval to find some sort of vocabulary control in force.

Perhaps the most useful of these many vocabulary control devices for descriptors either as index terms or subject headings are rules such as Daily's which call for a classified guide. This would mean that the same rules be employed in the classification index and hence the classification schedule as are used for the subject headings. The natural or inherent relationships between subject headings and classification have already been noted in regard to the processes of subject analysis and linguistic bases. "Every subject heading list presupposes a basis in classification either through category analysis or through reference to a real or an ideal classification, because that is the way we organize and clarify our knowledge."[51] Both Harry Dewey and Perreault discern a concept of alphabetical classification. Harry Dewey states,

> The subject headings of the dictionary catalog rarely provide hierarchical classification in practice, and in theory they never do. Instead, they provide alphabetical classification. It is not absolutely essential to use the term alphabetical classification, but it is useful to do so, if only to keep in mind that subject headings do classify. In this sense, the word "classify" is being used to mean "categorize."[52]

In a similar vein Perreault says,

> To operate with a classification, even an enumerative one without general categories, is (compared to operating with

an LC subject-heading catalog) like finding one's way across town with the aid of a map, as against asking directions at each street corner. In this sense we can exclude subject-headings from the domain of classification; but we should not forget that classification in this strict sense of *systematic* conceptual organization, and subject-headings in that of *alphabetical* conceptual organization, are search strategies both—and are thus subject to the same criteria.[53]

Jolley points out the danger of an inconsistent alphabetical classification developing if no systematic conceptual organization is present.

The cataloguer who draws up a list of subject headings must begin by acting as a classifier. He cannot hope to enumerate all possible specific headings within his subject except by a process of consecutive subdivision. The more thorough is his analysis of the relationships of different terms the more accurate will be his definitions and the greater will be their uniformity and consistence. . . . What Cutter makes clear is that he considers that the use of "a well-devised network of cross-references" gives the subject heading catalogue much of the character of a classified catalogue. The references from specific to comprehensive terms imply an hierarchical subordination which is a form of classification. Such references are usually drawn up as the occasion demands and they build up a hidden classification which is likely to be less full and consistent than a system of classification which has been explicitly developed on some more consistent and unified intellectual basis.[54]

An opposite view may be seen in the development of the subject headings for the Science and Technology Project at the Library of Congress.

We also knew that a subject heading list could be started without having to build as elaborate a foundation as is required for the construction of a classification.[55]

Farradane on the other hand states, "The standardization of terms is well safeguarded by the construction of a classification."[56] He continues in this vein as he attacks the usual development of thesauri.

For information retrieval the word 'thesaurus' has, however, been loosely used for a system of standardizing terms and avoiding synonyms, which would be better done by a cross-reference index, and for indicating higher and lower class terms (very arbitrarily), which would be much better done by a classification system. Furthermore, different thesaurus lists are being prepared by workers in different special subjects,

so that co-ordination of effort will soon be impossible. It
is clear that the thesaurus principle is entirely inadequate,
if not misleading, for information retrieval.[57]

The use of classification or categorization is not unusual in the development
of special subject headings lists and thesauri. Often thesauri have category
lists or trees in addition to an alphabetical array. Margaret Mann says of
Miss Clyde Pettus' *Subject Headings in Education*,

> Through her study of the broad subject Education Miss
> Pettus has furnished a scientific tool which insures a sys-
> tematic selection of subject headings while providing for
> the alphabetical arrangement of these headings. She has
> accomplished this by a thorough study of the whole subject
> field before selecting any of the terms under which specific
> subjects are to be listed. By distinguishing the broad headings
> from the more minute and grouping all in a logical arrange-
> ment she has given the cataloger a classified list of subject
> headings which may be used in a dictionary catalog.[58]

In her introduction Miss Pettus states,

> The present work is an attempt to provide a guide for selec-
> tion. A classified arrangement has been adopted, not that
> the headings will be so grouped in the catalog, but to
> enable the selector to see relationships and possible over-
> lappings before a choice is made.
>
> The headings are supplied with definitions for which the
> authorities are cited.[59]

It is of importance to this study that this list is both in a classified order and
contains lexical entries or definitions for the headings. These headings contain
both lexical and contextual meanings. Another use of classified descriptors is
found in Derek Langridge's method of book indexing.

> Instead of entries being filed alphabetically as they are made,
> they must be kept in a classified order until the end of the
> book is reached. At this stage each section must be examined
> for cross references and all desirable permutations made of
> compound terms. Only after this should the entries finally
> be rearranged in alphabetical order.[60]

The foregoing discussion appears to demonstrate possible important
relationships between subject headings and classification. The literature survey
revealed only one study dealing with the relationship between Library of
Congress subject headings and classification. This study is a part of Jean
Perreault's lengthy article "On Bibliography and Automation: or, How to
Reinvent the Catalog." Perreault compared three subclasses of philosophy in

both the subject heading list and the classification schedule. He used diagrams for the three areas of epistemology, ontology, and cosmology. He found that the subject headings and classification were basically two different systems. He posed the question "Why are not subject-headings and classification organized into one rather than two system(s)?"[61] As a result of this study as well as the remainder of this section of the literature survey the second hypothesis of this investigation appears to be worthy of objective study.

Classified Catalog and Chain Indexing

Vocabulary control used in the alphabetical subject index of a classified catalog is quite comparable if not identical with the type of vocabulary control that is or should be practiced in the index to a classification schedule. The major difference is that the alphabetical subject index to a classified catalog is usually generated from the subject holdings of a particular library rather than the entire subject ranges of a classification schedule. This area is of further interest because the index to a classified catalog does form a very special type of subject heading and one that does not have the normal space restraints of a document or unit card system. The relationship of chain indexing to the classified catalog is obvious and will be discussed later in this section.

Any library developing a classified catalog will meet the inherent linguistic problems of vocabulary control in the generation of the alphabetical index to classified catalog. Miss Herrick writes,

> As catalogers have always known as documentalists are constantly announcing, the level of retrieval efficiency is determined by the adequacy of the descriptor language. That is why it has seemed necessary to concentrate a major part of time and effort on our index terminology.[62]

One general principle of vocabulary control in a classified catalog may be found in the following statement on the terminology of index entries in a standard work on classified catalogs written by Jesse Shera and Margaret Egan.

> Choice of terms, as between scientific and popular for example, will depend upon the nature of the library and its clientele. Whether the policy of the library is to use scientific or popular terminology or not, the desirability of choosing at either level that term most frequently used or most familiar to the clientele should be emphasized. In many cases, perhaps in most libraries, both may be very desirable. The specialist will use a specialized vocabulary in his own specialization, but as he approached less familiar areas his vocabulary approaches that of the layman. Inasmuch as alternative terms may be used rather freely in the

subject index to the classified catalog, decisions reflect not
so much need to choose *one* term in preference to all others
but rather the possibility of referring to a number of terms
that would naturally occur to a given clientele.[63]

Miss Herrick similarly notes the greater vocabulary control which is present
in the classified catalog.

One of the surprising elements of classified catalog work is
the discovery that the terminology, which weighs like an
albatross on the cataloger in dictionary cataloging, is actually
something over which it is possible to have considerable
mastery. This point has been made before, but the first
realization of it is an exciting moment for a cataloger. One
uses the LC subject heading list only to the extent it is helpful, varying terminology as long as it does not violate basic
principles of subject headings, and the resultant flexibility
and sensitivity of approach is a delight. . . . I have freedom
to express inter-relationships and aspects of topics impossible
to bring out in traditional subject work.[64]

She further notes the removal of repetitive redundant headings reduces the
necessary number of cards in the classified catalog. "The dictionary subject
catalog's use of overlapping terms results in multiple entries that can be
avoided in a classified catalog."[65] It should also be pointed out that the
Boston University catalog uses L. C. subject heading whenever possible for
index terms.[66]

R. F. Kennedy finds distinctions between the classification schedule
index terms, subject headings and the terms for the alphabetical subject index
to the classified catalog.

The index to the 16th edition of Dewey is clear, well arranged
and, within the necessary limits of an index to a scheme, very
full. It may well serve as a guide in the compilation of a subject index to the catalogue. It should not, however, be
slavishly copied. . . . The Library of Congress *Subject
Headings* is not a satisfactory model, for, although it can
be used as a substitute for a general index to the Library of
Congress scheme of classification, it is primarily intended to
be a list of subject headings used in the dictionary catalogues
of the library. Lists of subject headings for a dictionary
catalogue are useful for suggesting synonums but they are
compiled on a totally different principle from the subject
index to a classification. The subjects in a dictionary catalogue are tied together by means of references; in the classified
catalogue like subjects are collocated and the necessity for
nearly all the subject references falls away.

The subject index serves a twofold purpose: it acts as a
link between the name of a subject and the number assigned
to it, and it provides a complementary classification by
bringing together the numbers for all aspects of a subject
dispersed throughout the scheme. . . . The index refers to
all aspects of a subject, thus making it possible for a reader
who wants all the literature on a subject, irrespective of
aspect, to find the complete holdings of the library on that
subject. It does not bring together all aspects of a subject;
it provides references to the numbers under which the various
aspects will be found in the subject catalogue. To this extent
it is complementary classification.[67]

This same principle of references in the alphabetical subject index to the
numbers or other form of notation in the classified catalog may be seen in
rule 12. of Jeannette Lynn and Zola Hilton's "A Code for Construction and
Maintenance of the Classified Catalog."

For each class number in the classified catalog establish one
or more corresponding synonymous subject headings. No
term in the subject index should refer to a class broader than
the term. Thus: class number = subject heading and subject
heading = class number.[68]

As one considers the result of a series of references developing in the
alphabetical subject index, the possibility of a natural chain index appears,
particularly if the above rule 12. is to be followed. It is, however, better to
deliberately develop a chain index in the alphabetical subject index rather
than to allow one to generate itself.

T. MacCallum Walker defines chain indexing as, "Subject-indexing as
a term and as a process is familair to all librarians; chain-indexing is simply
subject-indexing in which every stage or link of the chain is separately indexed."[69]
Thomas Caless gives a more detailed explanation.

In subject analysis, concepts in documents may be translated
into nouns, groups of nouns, nouns with relational words or
connectives, or combinations of all of these which may be
arranged hierarchically in classified order, or in reverse order,
which is called a chain index. If we select related pairs of
concepts from the classified string or the chain index, we
find that there is a certain predictability in the way the
concepts appear. The classified string of terms appear in
a general to special arrangement; the chain indexing terms
appear in a special to general arrangement.[70]

Ranganathan is normally considered to be the originator of chain indexing.
"We are indebted to Ranganathan for the method, which he introduced some

20 years ago (which goes to show how long improved methods take to establish themselves even in such a highly documented profession as librarianship; it has only now been brought into prominence by the *B. N. B.* since 1950)."[71] However it is interesting that Cutter's rule 187 seems to anticipate chain indexing.

> References are needed not merely to the specific from the general but to the general from the more general and to that from the most general. There must be a pyramid of references, and this can be made only by a final revision after the completion of the cataloging. The best method is to draw off in a single column a list of all the subject-headings that have been made, to write opposite them their including classes in a second column and the including classes of these in a third
> . column; then to write these classes as headings to cards and under them the subject that stood respectively opposite to them in the list, to arrange the cards alphabetically, verify the references, and supplement them by thinking of all likely subordinate headings and ascertaining whether they are in the catalog, and also by considering what an inquirer would like to be told or reminded of if he were looking up the subject under consideration.[72]

A more detailed discussion of chain indexing and the existing rules will be included in the introduction to chapter five of this work.

The value of chain indexing appears to be more than that of a system of vocabulary control. Mills states,

> Chain indexing, then, is a very powerful aid in achieving the major aims of the indexer of a classified sequence, which are: firstly, to make sure that every keyword (i.e., every term likely to be consulted by the readers of the library concerned) is indexed (i.e., appears as the first word of some entry); secondly, because of the numerous ways in which many subjects can be indexed, to do this *systematically*, so as to avoid doubt and inconsistency on he part of the indexer; thirdly, to do this *economically*, avoiding superfluous entries by recognizing that many of the pathways to the location of information are provided by the classified sequence itself, *and need not be repeated in the alphabetical index.*[73]

He further sees the chain index as a device to reveal relationships between subjects or to be a fully developed relative index.[74] In this sense he believes the chain index represents an alphabetical classification system.[75] D. W. Doughty states, "To the cataloguer, a particular virtue of chain procedure is that, once the class number has been determined, it is a virtually automatic procedure;"[76] and, Tom Wiison points out ". . . you have nothing to lose but your 'see' and 'see also' references."[77]

It should be observed that the chain indexing of classification schedules often varies in relation to the necessary revision of the schedule terminology as a result of the notation of the classification. As long as the notation is perfectly hierarchical or sequential most of the vocabulary will be utilized. It may also be seen at this point that if the vocabulary control necessary for chain indexing could be previously applied to the construction of the classification schedule then no major modification of schedule terms would be necessary. This possibility could directly lead to the use of the chain index in place of subject headings.

On the other hand the development of the chain index can be most helpful even if terminology changes are necessary. Coates observes that,

> Whereas in chain procedural indexing to the Colon scheme, the subject indexer can virtually limit the field of his concern to the digits of the notation, in applying the technique to the Decimal Classification he must maintain a close watch on the classification schedule of terms as well. This critical appraisal of the classification schedule may at first sight seem to involve a great deal of work for the subject indexer: but it is actually the work which the classifier must perform in order to classify. So that if classification and subject indexing are carried out as a unitary operation, there will be no superfluity of effort. In fact, chain procedure is an excellent and necessary check on the possibility of the classifier's jumping of mental fences out of turn.[78]

From this last quotation we may discern the fullest possible subject integration. By the use of a chain index, classification and subject indexing do become a unitary coordinated process.

However it should be acknowledged that chain indexing has its critics also. John Sharp states,

> Faceted classification with chain indexing has been advocated as a solution to the problem of dealing with complex subjects, and it is undoubtedly easier to assign a synthetic notation than it is to place a complex subject in an enumerative classification scheme, but the point is that finding the complex subject for retrieval is not one wit [sic] easier. It is very difficult to understand why such store has been set by these methods, and there is now some realisation of their shortcomings.[79]

Other critics include British classificationists D. J. Foskett,[80] Farradane[81] and Jean Aitchison.[82]

One principle exponent of chain indexing is the *British National Bibliography*. It too has been criticized. Columbia University Professor Theodore Hines writes, "It should be recognized that the index will be as useful as the subject headings in the dictionary catalog for this purpose only if the entries are specific subject entries, not if the index is, in effect, only a index to the class schedules or generated, as in the British National Bibliography, in some mysterious way from the schedules."[83] He is quickly answered by Britisher Wilson, "But the only excuse anyone can offer for considering chain indexing a 'mysterious method' is ignorance."[84] Scheerer praises the *B. N. B.* for its use of chain indexing.

> Because the subject headings in the *BNB* are derived through the classification and becuase the books are arranged in logical order, the Index has the advantage of guiding the reader to any one book upon several subject levels. It works in this way: When a book is subject-analyzed and classified, the numbers on broader subject levels above it are "charged" in the classification schedule and are indexed, even though they may display no books at the time. The reader taking the general approach, as many do, is then led to the immediate area where the specific book he really wants is listed. On the contrary, if he takes the specific approach and does not find at that number enough material for his needs, he will find in the immediate area the general works that include his specific topic. Thus there are always two types of approach, the direct and the indirect.[85]

Further in this vein Coates says,

> We may now make an attempt to draw some general con- clusions on the exploitation of classification on behalf of the alphabetico-specific catalogue. In the first place, chain procedureal analysis of the position of a subject within a classification scheme can provide the verbal raw material for the subject heading and for the chain of references leading down to it. In order to extract this material com- petently, the subject cataloguer must refer directly to the real hierarchical structure of the classification schedule, and not merely to the ingredients of the notation: he must also be able to elaborate the published schedule in order to specify subjects not provided for by the classi- fication maker, but he need not elaborate the notation.[86]

It must be emphasized that chain indexing is the obvious key to complete subject analysis containing integrated terms of descriptors for both index and classification, both subject heading and classification, both classification index and subject heading. However, it must be observed that the converse of the last part of Coates concept may also occur. That is to say that the classification schedule may go to greater depth or specificity than the list of subjects or descriptors involved. In such a case the list of subjects would then need to be elaborated. Finally it is most important to exercise vocabulary control with great care at this point.

The applicability of chain indexing to L. C. classification is the concluding section of this portion of the literature search. First it may be noted that L. C. classification has served the classified catalog of Boston University well. Miss Herrick writes,

> The quarterly revisions, the specificity, and the flexibility
> of the LC are all important factors in any consideration of
> its usefulness in a classified catalog. As has been noted, Boston
> University presents the only testing of the LC in a classified
> catalog untilizing all fields of knowledge. The test is in its
> sixteenth year, and we are constantly delighted at the
> possibilities of the LC. . . . the classification system does
> work and does provide adequate hospitality for an over-
> increasing range of subject concepts, both simple and
> complex.[87]

Second although L. C. classification does not use an hierarchical notation, Mills feels the notation is indexable.

> An obvious difference here is that the notation is largely
> arithmetical—so its numbers never show subordination.
> Therefore the preliminary casting into its hierarchy of
> the subjects to be indexed can only be done by examining
> the layout of the schedules, observing the indention and
> heavy type by which subordination is displayed and checking
> by the printed index (which should never be neglected as
> a source of information in this respect, whatever scheme is
> used).[88]

Third it may be noted that even if L. C. classification is a defective classification system as some writers believe, even a defective classification can be chain indexed. Mills states,

> Do defects in the classification hinder chain indexing? As
> a procedure for constructing an index, very little. The
> terms which go into the index are not dependent on the
> schedules, and if the latter provides inadequately detailed
> subdivision the indexer simply indexes the further stages
> of division to the number for the last scheduled step. But
> the economies of chain indexing rest partly on the assump-
> tion that the classified sequence is itself easily followed
> through a limited number of steps (e.g., from Engineering
> to Radio Engineering); if the chain is not clear, due to
> defects in the structure of the classification, then the
> post-indexing step is to that extent less efficient. But
> no method of alphabetical indexing will remedy defective
> classification.[89]

Perreault even admits, "LC is for the shelves alone, for all practical purposes (though any system, after all, can have chain indexing attached to it)."[90] As a result of this section of the literature search, it appears that the third hypothesis is worthy of objective consideration.

Conclusion

Resulting directly from the foregoing literature survey and the additional sources included in chapter one, the tentative hypotheses of this investigation may be restated as the formal hypotheses.

The first hypothesis of this study is that the indexes for individual Library of Congress classification schedules vary in fullness and represents something other than a single logical development.

The second hypothesis of this study is that there is a discernible relationship, demonstrated by a high percentage of identity, between the terminology of the L. C. subject headings and the L. C. classification.

The third hypothesis is that the use of chain procedure indexing will unify the vocabulary of the Library's subject cataloging so that an alphabetical array of the classification will be a list of subject headings and that a classified array of subject headings will be the classification schedule. It may be that the test of the third hypothesis will justify such a statement as Scheerer's.

> Instead of "subject-heading" the book under two or more
> large, non-descriptive, and pretty useless terms, as we now
> do , the cataloger who uses the formula phrase type of heading
> can specify the real subject of the book and its phase relations.
> . . . The present need is not for more subject heading lists but
> for a sound method.[91]

And it may provide the complete verbal access desired by Raimund E. Matthis.

> Rather than suggesting that libraries remain with or move
> to a more elaborative system of notation, librarians should
> more practically work to develop a "complete" verbal
> access to collections and forget quixotic dreams of total
> classificatory systems which will let computers vomit
> endless print-outs of near useless material.[92]

DATA COLLECTION METHODS

Descriptive Analysis of the Individual L. C. Indexes

The first hypothesis will be tested by the following method. A representative range of class numbers will be selected in each L. C. schedule containing an index. This investigator will choose a short range of numbers such as a page or two which hopefully contains the representative type of material covered by the schedule. For example, in the schedule covering subclasses PN: General literature, PR: English literature, PS: American literature, and PZ: Fiction in English and Juvenile literature, I have tested the sections on Anglo-Saxon literature. Because of the arrangement of this schedule the history and criticism of literature is separated from collections of literature as well as from individual authors and works. For example PR 145-236 is the range of numbers tested for history and criticism of Anglo-Saxon literature and PR 1490-1530 for collections of Anglo-Saxon literature as well as the beginning of the range for individual Anglo-Saxon authors and works. This choice is representative as it does cover the three basic types of material in this schedule, i.e., history and criticism of literature, collections of literature, and individual authors and works. After choosing the range of numbers these numbers are searched for in the alphabetical indexes. This operation includes scanning the indexes as well as looking up in the indexes each pertinent schedule term. Next these numbers as found in the indexes will be rearranged in an extracted alphabetical order. Finally these numbers will be rearranged in classed order to be compared with the original representative ranges.

Descriptive Analysis of the Relationship Between L. C. Subject Headings and L. C. Classification

The second hypothesis will be tested by the following method. An array of random numbers will be used to select subject headings from the L. C. list of subject headings. The Rand Corporation's *A Million Random Digits with 100,000 Normal Deviates* will be used in determining the random sample. Following the recommended procedure for determining a starting place a serial number will be chosen. As there are 1432 pages in the list of subject headings and three columns per page in the list, the first four digits of each appropriate random number will be used in determining the page and column containing the heading. These four digits will be divided by the number of columns in the subject heading list to give the exact page and column for the heading. The four digits will be treated as a whole number at this point. If there is no fractional remainder, then the first column on the page whose number is given as a result of the division will be used. If there is a fraction of two thirds, the third column will be used. As a result of this method of application of the random numbers, all numbers higher than "42989" cannot be used. The last digit of the original random number will be read in inches down the column. The length of a column in the list is approximately 10 inches. If there is no subject heading at the point of measure, first an additional inch down will be read, then an additional inch up until a subject heading is reached.

Once the random subject heading is discerned, the following processes will be employed to collect the data. First the random heading will be

39

recorded and numbered, e. g. SH 1, SH 2, etc. This phase in the data collection concerns itself solely with the subject heading and its relation to the classification heading(s) and the index heading(s). If the subject heading has a classification number indicated in its entry, this number serves as the access point to the classification schedule. If the random subject heading does not have a classification number as part of its entry, the subject heading will be searched in the seemingly appropriate classification schedules. The form of the classification heading(s) will be recorded next to the subject heading. Next the subject heading will be searched in the index of the schedule in hand. The result of this search will be similarly recorded. Thus for each SH factor (subject heading) there could be at least one classification heading (CH) and one index heading (IH).

The second phase of the data collection concerns the remainder of subject heading entry. All the references and subdivisions and subsubdivisions of the subject heading will be collected. The syndetic structure of the subject heading includes the possibility of *sa* headings, *x* headings, and *xx* headings. There are four potential parts for each heading in the second phase. First all the *sa* headings will be recorded. If they have classification numbers given in their own entries, these numbers will be recorded and used as access to the classification schedules. All CH's and IH.s will be recorded. If there is no classification number given for a *sa* heading then the *sa* heading will be searched in the index to the schedule used in the first phase. If there is no entry in the index the appropriate pages of the classification schedules will be scanned for the related classification heading. If it seems advisable to refer to a different classification schedule, this will also be done. After all the *sa* headings and their related CH and IH headings are recorded, all *x* headings will be recorded. As the *x* headings would not have classification numbers in the subject heading list, these will be searched directly in the index to the classification schedule. Also the classification tables will be scanned if necessary. The last of the syndetic devices to be considered will be the *xx* headings. These will be treated in a very similar fashion to that already described for the *sa* headings. The fourth part of this phase will deal with any subdivisions of the subject heading. If these subdivisions have classification numbers, the related heading in the schedule will be immediately discerned; if not, then the subdivision will be searched in the classification index and scanned in the tables if necessary.

Experimental Models and Formulation of Rules for Chain Indexing

The third hypothesis will be tested by the following method. The experimental models will result from sections of the classification chosen by the investigator. This investigator proposes to choose an area in which he is both familiar and knowledgeable. As each term is indexed Daily's *Rules*[93] will be applied for form and necessary chain indexing rules will be formulated. For example the following term from schedule *PN, PR, PS, PZ* "syntax"

PR 3078 refers to Shakespeare's syntax. There are the following hierarchical links in this chain:

P	Philology and literature
PR	English literature
PR2199-3195	English renaissance (1500-1640)
PR2411-3195	The drama
PR2417-3195	Individual authors
PR2750-3112	Shakespeare, William
PR2965-3088	Criticism and interpretation
PR3072-3088	Language
PR3075-3081	Grammar
PR3078	Syntax

The following index terms could result:

SYNTAX: SHAKESPEARE, PR 3078
GRAMMAR: SHAKESPEARE, PR 3075-3081
LANGUAGE: CRITICISM: SHAKESPEARE, PR 3072-3088
CRITICISM: SHAKESPEARE, PR 2965-3088
Interpretation: SHAKESPEARE, PR 2965-3088
SHAKESPEARE, WILLIAM, PR 2750-3112
DRAMA: ENGLISH LITERATURE, PR 2411-3195
ENGLISH LITERATURE, PR
PHILOLOGY, P
Literature, P

A basic rule may be formulated from this example. IF THE CONTEXTUAL MEANING OF A TERM IS DEPENDENT ON THE LOCATION OF THAT TERM IN THE CLASSIFIED ARRAY, THE MOST SPECIFIC HIERARCHICAL TERM THAT WILL SUPPLY THAT CONTEXT MUST BE ADDED AS A CONTEXTUAL LINK FOLLOWING THE INDEX TERM. This is done in the case of "syntax", "grammar", "language", etc. It is not done for "Shakespeare, William" as the assumed context and the classificatory reference of the name is specifically "English literature". "English renaissance" and "Individual authors" may be considered as *unsought* links. The problem of unsought links will be discussed in chapter five.

All of the rules formulated in the experimental phase will then be applied and tested by deriving samples from the second descriptive phase. The new subject *ascriptors* derived from the chain indexing will be compared with the present subject headings as a test of the third hypothesis. Ambiguity and redundancy will be treated in this test as in the second descriptive phase. Near synonyms will also be considered.

DEFINITION OF TERMS

Descriptive Analysis of the Individual L. C. Indexes

An access term is any entry in the index. It may refer to a specific number, a specific range of numbers, a general range of numbers (i.e., a class or a subclass), a general reference, or a specific cross reference. Further the type of subdivision in the access terms is the same as the four possible subdivisions of an L. C. class number, i.e., general form divisions, geographical divisions, chronological divisions, and specific subject subdivisions.

A schedule term refers to all distinctive terms or phrases on the page of the classification schedule.

Adequate structure means that an access term is entered under all pertinent parts.

Inadequate structure means that some pertinent parts should be rotated to entry position.

Descriptive Analysis of the Relationship Between L. C. Subject Headings and L. C. Classification

All of the linguistic terms used in this study are taken from the writings of H. A. Gleason,[94] Roderick A. Jacobs and Peter S. Rosenbaum,[95] Francis P. Dinneen[96] and Noam Chomsky.[97] The use of linguistic method and terminology is based on the patterns and practices used by Jay E. Daily in his "The Grammar of Subject Headings."[98]

Near synonyms are terms with the same or closely related lexical meanings.

Ambiguous headings are subject headings with more than one classificatory reference.

Classificatory references are the L. C. classification numbers listed after the subject headings in the L. C. list.

Redundant headings are subject headings which receive the same classificatory references.

Code of terms used in the tables in this section:

SH	=	subject heading
CH	=	classification heading
IH	=	index heading
W	=	a noun in mass form
W_a	$\equiv$	an adjectival word
F	=	a function word
F_c	=	a conjunctive function word
f	=	an article function word
(sp)	=	a spelling variation
$-Z_1$	=	a count noun in the singular

Experimental Model and Formulation of Rules for Chain Indexing

Unsought links are hierarchical links in a chain index that result in entry terms unlikely to be useful to the user.

Missing links are hierarchical links in a chain index that are not present in the classification schedule and/or the notation.

False links are notational links that do not represent any classificatory hierarchy.

Contextual links are hierarchical links added to index terms to retain the classificatory context.

Ascriptors are index terms derived from chain indexing.

[1] Immroth, *op. cit.*, pp. 24-28; 49-56; 86-88; 297-308.

[2] James Duff Brown, *Library Classification and Cataloguing* (London: Grafton & Co., 1916), pp. 95-96.

[3] John Metcalfe, *Alphabetical Subject Indication of Information*, Rutgers Series on Systems for the Intellectual Organization of Information, Vol. III (New Brunswick, N. J.: Graduate School of Library Service, Rutgers, the State University, 1965), p. 139.

[4] Frederick Jonker, *Indexing Theory, Indexing Methods and Search Devices* (New York: The Scarecrow Press, Inc., 1964), pp. 61-62.

[5] Coates, *Subject Catalogues, loc. cit.*

[6] Sayers, *op. cit.*, p. 81.

[7] Mills, *A Modern Outline, op. cit.*, p. 81.

[8] B. C. Vickery, *Classification and Indexing in Science* (2d ed., enl.; London: Butterworths, 1959), p. 49.

[9] Sayers, *op. cit.*, p. 75.

[10] John Metcalfe, *Subject Classifying and Indexing of Libraries and Literature* (New York: The Scarecrow Press, Inc., 1959), p. 125.

[11] "Melvil Dewey's Introduction," *Dewey Decimal Classification and Relative Index*, Devised by Melvil Dewey (Ed. 17; Lake Placid Club, N. Y.: Forest Press, Inc. of Lake Placid Club Education Foundation, 1965), I, 67.

[12] Benjamin Custer, "Editor's Introduction," *Dewey Decimal Classification and Relative Index*, Devised by Melvil Dewey (Ed. 17; Lake Placid Club, N. Y.: Forest Press, Inc. of Lake Placid Club Education Foundation, 1965), I, 33.

[13] Mills, *A Modern Outline, op. cit.*, p. 54.

[14] Mills, "Chain Indexing and the Classified Catalogue," *op. cit.*, p. 142.

[15] Brown, *op. cit.*, pp. 59-60.

[16] Custer, *op. cit.*, pp. 34-35.

[17] Brown, *op. cit.*, p. 99.

[18] Coates, *Subject Catalogues, op. cit.*, pp. 89-90.

[19] S. R. Ranganathan, *Colon Classification*, Ranganathan Series in Library Science, 4; Madras Library Association Publishing Series, 26 (New York: Asia Publishing House, 1963), pp. 2.124-2.172.

[20] *Supra*, p. 12.

[21] Mary Darrah Herrick, "Classified Catalog at Boston University, 1948-1964," *Library Resources & Technical Services,* VIII (Summer, 1964), 293.

[22] Desmond Taylor, "Reclassification to LC: Planning and Personnel," In *Reclassification, Rationale and Problems.* Proceedings of a Conference on Reclassification held at the Center of Adult Education, University of Maryland, College Park, April 4 to 6, 1968. (College Park: School of Library and Information Services, 1968), p. 98.

[23] Phyllis A. Richmond, "General Advantages and Disadvantages of Using the Library of Congress Classification," in *The Use of the Library of Congress Classification,* edited by Richard H. Schimmelpfeng and C. Donald Cook, (Chicago: American Library Association, 1969), p. 214.

[24] Jonker, *op. cit.,* p. 20.

[25] Kent, *op. cit.,* p. 113.

[26] George Scheerer, "Subject Catalog Examined," *Library Quarterly,* XXVII (July 1957), 192.

[27] Jolley, *op. cit.,* p. 100.

[28] Scheerer, *op. cit.,* p. 188.

[29] Julia Pettee, *Subject Headings, the History and Theory of the Alphabetical Subject Approach to Books,* (New York: The H. W. Wilson Co., 1946).

[30] David Judson Hayking, *Subject Headings, A Practical Guide* (Washington: Government Printing Office, 1951).

[31] Oliver Linton Lilley, "Terminology, Form, Specificity and the Syndetic Structure of Subject Headings for English Literature" (unpublished D.L.S. dissertation, School of Library Service, Columbia University, 1958).

[32] Charles Ammi Cutter, *Rules for a Dictionary Catalog,* U. S. Bureau of Education, Special Report on Public Libraries—Part II (4th ed., rewritten; Washington: Government Printing Office, 1904), p. 66.

[33] Mills, *A Modern Outline, op. cit.,* p. 175.

[34] H. T. Dewey, "Relationships between the Headings in the Subject Catalog and the Classification Numbers of the Books," in *Reclassification: Rationale and Problems, op. cit.,* p. 66.

[35] Jean M. Perreault, ed., *Reclassification, Rationale and Problems, op. cit.,* p. 56.

[36] Paul S. Dunkin, *Cataloging U. S. A.* (Chicago: American Library Association, 1969), p. 73.

[37] Jean M. Perreault, *Re-Classification: Some Warnings and a Proposal,* no. 87 (Urbana: University of Illinois Graduate School of Library Science, 1967), p. 8.

[38] Scheerer, *op. cit.,* p. 192.

[39] Jay E. Daily, "Many Changes, No Alterations: An Analysis of Library of Congress Subject Headings, Seventh Edition," *Library Journal,* XCII (November 1, 1967), 3961-3962.

[40] Dunkin, *op. cit.,* p. 84.

[41] John Farradane, "The Challenge of Information Retrieval," *Journal of Documentation,* XVII (December 1961), 236.

[42] Coates, *Subject Catalogues, op. cit.,* p. 175.

[43] John Farradane, "Fundamental Fallacies and New Needs in Classification," in *The Sayers Memorial Volume* (London: The Library Association, 1961), p. 121.

[44] Perreault, *Re-Classification: Some Warnings, op. cit.,* p. 16.

[45] Vickery, *op. cit.,* p. 77.

[46] Cutter, *op. cit.,* pp. 66-77.

[47] Jay E. Daily, "The Grammar of Subject Headings; a Formulation of Rules for Subject Headings Based on a Syntactical and Morphological Analysis of the Library of Congress List" (unpublished D.L. S. dissertation, School of Library Service, Columbia University, 1957), pp. 152-161.

[48] John Metcalfe, "Tentative Code of Rules for Alphabetica-specific Entry," *Subject Classifying and INdexing of Libraries and Literature, op. cit.,* pp. 262-292.

[49] Marie Prevost, "An Approach to Theory and Method in General Subject Heading," *Library Quarterly,* XVI (1946), 140.

[50] Scheerer, *op. cit.,* p. 198.

[51] *Ibid.,* p. 192.

[52] H. T. Dewey, *op. cit.,* p. 67.

[53] Perreault, *Re-Classification: Some Warnings, op. cit.,* p. 13.

[54] Jolley, *op. cit.,* p. 104.

[55] C. D. Gull, "Some Remarks on Subject Headings," *Special Libraries,* XL (March 1949), 83.

[56] Farradane, "The Challenge of Information Retrieval," *loc. cit.*

[57] *Ibid.,* p. 237.

[58] Margaret Mann, "Preface," in *Subject Headings in Education: A Systematic List for Use in a Dictionary Catalog,* by Clyde Pettus. (New York: The H. W. Wilson Co., 1938), p. vii.

[59] Clyde Pettus, *Subject Headings in Education: A Systematic List for Use in a Dictionary Catalog.* With a preface by Margaret Mann (New York: The H. W. Wilson Co., 1938), pp. xi-xii.

[60] Derek Langridge, "Classification and Book Indexing," in *The Sayers Memorial Volume.* (London: The Library Association, 1961), p. 192.

[61] Perreault, "On Bibliography and Automation," *loc. cit.*

[62] Herrick, "Classified Catalog," *op. cit.,* p. 297.

[63] Jesse H. Shera and Margaret Egan, *The Classified Catalog, Basic Principals and Practices,* With a Code for the Construction and Maintenance of the Classified Catalog, by Jeannette M. Lynn and Zola Hilton (Chicago: American Library Association, 1956), p. 75.

[64] Herrick, "Classified Catalog," *op. cit.,* pp. 291-292.

[65] Herrick, "Development of a Classified Catalog for a University Library," *College & Research Libraries,* XIV (October 1953), 423.

[66] *Ibid.,* p. 418.

[67] R. F. Kennedy, *Classified Cataloguing, a Practical Guide* (Cape Town: A. A. Balkema, 1966), pp. 31-33.

[68] Jeannette M. Lynn and Zola Hilton, "A Code for the Construction and Maintenance of the Classified Catalog," in *The Classified Catalog, Basic Principles,* by Jesse H. Shera and Margaret Egan (Chicago: American Library Association, 1956), p. 92.

[69] MacCallum Walker, *op. cit.,* p. 261.

[70] Thomas Caless, "Preconditions of Electronic Searchability," in *Reclassification, Rationale and Problems, op. cit.,* p. 179.

[71] Mills, "Chain Indexing," *loc. cit.*

[72] Cutter, *op. cit.,* p. 79.

[73] Mills, "Indexing a Classification Scheme," *Indexer,* II (Autumn 1960), 44.

[74] Mills, "Chain Indexing," *op. cit.,* p. 141.

[75] Mills, "Indexing a Classification Scheme," *op. cit.,* p. 41.

[76] D. W. Doughty, "Chain Procedure Subject Indexing and Featuring a Classified Catalogue," *Library Association Record,* LVII (May, 1955), 177.

[77] Tom Wilson, "Chain Indexing Is Not Mysterious," *Library Journal,* LXXXVIII (January 15, 1963), 190.

[78] Coates, *Subject Catalogues, op. cit.,* p. 116.

[79] John R. Sharp, *Some Fundamentals of Information Retrieval,* (New York: London House & Maxwell, 1965), p. 91.

[80] D. J. Foskett, "Two Notes on Indexing Techniques," *Journal of Documentation,* XVIII (December, 1962), 188.

[81] Farradane, "The Challenge of Information Retrieval," *loc. cit.*

[82] Jean Aitchison, "English Electric Company," *Classification Research Group Bulletin* No. 7 in *Journal of Documentation,* XVIII (June 1962), 80-88.

[83] Theodore C. Hines, "Revolution in Public Library Cataloging," *Library Journal,* LXXXVII (May 1, 1962), 727.

[84] Wilson, *op. cit.,* p. 189.

[85] Scheerer, *op. cit.,* p. 189.

[86] Coates, *Subject Catalogues, op. cit.,* pp. 145-146.

[87] Herrick, "Classified Catalog," *op. cit.,* p. 298.

[88] Mills, "Chain Indexing," *op. cit.,* p. 146.

[89] International Federation for Documentation. *Proceedings of the International Study Conference on Classification for Information Retrieval,* held at Beatrice Webb House, Dorking, England, 13-17th May 1957 (London: ASLIB: New York: Pergamon Press, 1957), p. 104.

[90] Perreault, *Reclassification, Rationale and Problems, op. cit.,* p. 81.

[91] Scheerer, *op. cit.,* p. 196.

[92] Perreault, *Reclassification, Rationale and Problems, op. cit.,* pp. 28-29.

[93] *Supra,* p. 28.

[94] H. A. Gleason, *An Introduction to Descriptive Linguistics,* (rev. ed.,; New York: Holt, Rinehart and Winston, 1961).

[95] Roderick A. Jacobs and Peter S. Rosenbaum, *English Transformational Grammar* With an Epilogue by Paul S. Postal, A Blaisdell Book in the Humanities (Waltham, Mass.: Blaisdell Publishing Co., 1968).

[96] Francis P. Dinneen, *An Introduction to General Linguistics* (New York: Holt, Rinehart and Winston, Inc., 1967).

[97] Noam Chomsky, *Aspects of the Theory of Syntax* (Cambridge, Mass.: The M.I.T. Press, 1965); *Current Issues in Linguistic Theory* (The Hague: Mouton, 1969); *Language and Mind* (New York: Harcourt, Brace & World, Inc., 1968); *Syntactic Structures* (The Hague: Mouton, 1968); *Topics in the Theory of Generative Grammar* (The Hague: Mouton, 1969).

[98] *Supra,* fn. 47.

CHAPTER III

DEVELOPMENT OF THE ARGUMENT
FOR ANALYSIS OF L. C. INDEXES

ANALYSIS OF THE DATA COLLECTED

The data collected has been analyzed for the three following elements:
1) index terms, 2) class numbers, and 3) Cutter numbers. Indexability has
been concerned with what was indexed, what was not indexed, and any
correlations of these two. Each of these elements may be considered in regard
to both the index and the schedule. Index terms in the index have been
defined as access terms and have been tabulated for each range of numbers
selected in the individual schedules. Similarly the index terms in the schedules
have been defined as schedule terms and have been counted for each range.
Class numbers within each range have been counted in both the index and
the schedule as have the Cutter numbers. For instance within the range of
numbers NA 6800-7020 assigned to "Buildings for recreation" there are the
following 22 access terms in the index. First those access terms which fit
into the specific range of numbers NA 6800-7020 are given in classified order.

> Casino buildings: NA 6810.
> Music-halls: NA 6820-40.
> Opera houses: NA 6820-40.
> Theaters (Architecture): NA 6820-40.
> Panorama buildings: NA 6850.
> Amphitheatres: NA 6860.
> Stadia (Architecture): NA 6860.
> Grand stands: NA 6870.
> Coliseums: NA 6880.
> Convention halls: NA 6880.
> Lecture halls: NA 6880.
> Ice palaces: NA 6890.
> Boat-houses: NA 6920.
> Park buildings: NA 6930.
> Baths
>   Public: NA 7010.
> Public comfort stations: NA 7020.

The next group of access terms represent specific cross references contained
within this range of numbers.

Theaters (Architecture): NA 6820-40.
　　Greek: NA 278.T5
　　Roman: NA 325.T5
　　Restaurant architecture: NA 7855.

The last group of access terms in this example are inappropriate references which should refer to this specific range of numbers but do not.

Contracts and specifications, Architectural: NA 2640-5
Houses (Architecture): NA 7100-8480.
Public buildings: NA 4170-4510.

In the schedule for this same range of numbers NA 6800-7020 there are a minimum of 43 indexable schedule terms. In the following example those schedule terms which are indexed are in italics. Only 51 percent of these 43 schedule terms are indexed by the previously listed 22 access terms.

NA
Buildings for recreation.
　　Under each:
　　　(6) Contracts and specifications.
6800 General
6810 *Casinos.*
　　Theaters. Opera houses. Music halls.
　　　General works.
6820　　Before 1800.
6821　　1801-
6826　　*Contracts* and specifications.
6830　　United States.
　　　Special cities.
6840 Foreign countries, A-Z.
　　　e.g.　.F6　France.
　　　　　.F7　　Paris.
　　　　　.F8　　　Opera house.
　　　　　.F81-98　　Other special.
　　Greek *theaters,* see NA 278.T5.
　　Roman *theaters,* see Na 325.T5.
6850 *Panoramas.*
6860 *Amphitheaters. Stadia.*
6870 *Grand stands.*
6880 *Convention halls, coliseums, lecture halls,* etc.
6890 *Ice palaces.*
　　Bowling alleys, see GV 909.
　　Gymnasiums, see GV 405.
　　Rinks, see GV 848-851.
6920 *Boat houses.*
　　　Cf. NA 7970
　　Riding halls, see SF 310.
6930 *Park buildings.*
　　Other *public buildings.*
　　　Restaurants, see NA 7855.

7010 *Baths* and wash houses.
7020 *Public comfort stations.*

There are 17 class numbers within this example: NA 6800, 6810, 6820, 6821, 6826, 6830, 6835, 6840, 6850, 6860, 6870, 6880, 6890, 6920, 6930, 7010, and 7020. In addition there are four Cutter numbers: NA 6840.F6, .F7, .F8, and .F81-98. Of the 22 access terms there are only 11 class numbers in the index or 65 percent of the 17 class numbers in the schedule. None of the four Cutter numbers are indexed.

The example of the range of numbers NA 6800-7020 has been used to demonstrate the basic analysis which has been applied to sections of each of the L. C. schedules with indexes. In addition, these six areas of access terms, schedule terms, class numbers, class numbers indexed, Cutter numbers, and Cutter numbers indexed have been further analyzed when appropriate in regard to specific class numbers, specific ranges of class numbers, general ranges of class numbers, general references, specific cross references and inappropriate references. Specific class numbers are individual class numbers which are represented verbally by a word or a series of words. In the previous examples "NA 6850 Panoramas" is a specific class number in both the schedule and the index. Specific ranges of class numbers are ranges of individual class numbers contained within the sample. "Opera houses: NA 6820-40" is an instance of a specific range of class numbers. It may be noted that this instance only occurs in the index. General ranges of class numbers are ranges of class numbers extending beyond the specific range of the sample. For instance in the range of numbers SF 361-415 "Animal culture: SF" is an example of a general range of class numbers. General references are directions applicable to various sections of the classification. In the range of numbers Z 2000-2049 "Bibliography, see also National bibliography, Personal bibliography, Subject bibliography; also Biobibliography, Catalogs" is a general reference. Specific cross references are directions applicable to another specific number or range of numbers wither within or outside of the sample. "Riding halls, see SF 310" is a specific cross reference. Inappropriate references are directions to non-existent class numbers. Index references which fail to include an appropriate reference to the sample being investigated are also considered to be inappropriate references. Examples of this have already been displayed as part of the 22 access terms in the sample for NA 6800-7020. In addition, the type of subdivisions of each of these six areas has been considered in regard to general form divisions, geographical divisions, chronological divisions, and specific subject subdivisions. "NA 6800 General" is an example of a general form division; "NA 6830 United States" is a geographical division; "NA 6820 General works. Before 1800" is a chronological division; and, "NA 6810 Casinos" is an example of a specific subject subdivision.

Each sample will be considered in relation to the above description. First, the justification for choosing each sample is 1) if a schedule has a discernible repetitive pattern in its internal organization, a representative sample of that pattern has been chosen; or, 2) if no repetitive pattern can be discerned, an apparently typical page has been selected. Second, the correlation by a simple arithmetic percentage of the schedule terms and access terms is cited as well as similar correlations for class numbers and Cutter numbers. Third, the variations of specific class numbers, specific ranges of class numbers, general ranges, etc. is considered in relation to index terms, class numbers and Cutter numbers. Fourth, any meaningful correlations resulting from the analysis by subdivisions is presented. Fifth, the syntactical structure of the access terms in the index itself is discussed. Sixth, a general identity figure for the number itself of terms appearing in identical graphemic form in the index and the schedule is given. After each sample has been analysed in the text, a summary table of the analysis for that sample will be given. After all the samples have been presented, a complete summary total will be given. This summary total should serve as a natural bridge between the analysis section of this chapter and the interpretation and conclusion section of this chapter.

A: General works, Polygraphy
There is no index to this schedule.

B, pt. 1, B-BJ: Philosophy
B 1-128 is used because this range of numbers contains general and specific headings for philosophy as well as including individual philosophers. As may be observed in Table 1 55 access terms or 35% of 156 schedule terms are indexed in this sample. Twenty-five class numbers or 37% of 67 class numbers in the sample are indexed and 14 Cutter numbers or 58% of 24 Cutter numbers are indexed. It may also be observed in Table 1 that specific ranges of numbers are used with more frequency in the index than in the schedule. Further it may be noted that of 41 specific subject subdivisions, 34 or 83% are indexed. The structure of the access terms considered separately shows that 40 terms are adequately entered in the index with no rotation or permutation needed to provide maximum access. Fifteen access terms appear to need rotation. Finally, the number of schedule terms appearing in identical graphemic form in the index is 22. This is 14% of the total schedule terms (156) in this range of numbers.

TABLE 1 — SUMMARY ANALYSIS OF B 1-128

	Access Terms	Schedule Terms	Class Nos.	Class Nos. Indexed	Cutter Nos.	Cutter Nos. Indexed
Total	55	156	67	25	24	14
Specific Class Numbers	37	148	63	16	21	12
Specific Ranges of Class Numbers	17	4	4	9	3	2
General Ranges of Class Numbers	0	3	—	—	—	—
General References	0	0	—	—	—	—
Specific Cross References	1	1	—	—	—	—
Inappropriate References	0	0	—	—	—	—
General Form Divisions	15	59	26	12	9	0
Geographical Divisions	4	50	30	3	4	0
Chronological Subdivisions	2	6	4	1	0	0
Specific Subject Subdivisions	34	41	7	9	11	14

B, pt. 2, BL-BX: Religion

The range of numbers for the Bible in English, BS 125-198, is selected as being representative of the many different categories of material in this schedule. There are general headings in the sample as well as specific headings for names and versions of the Bible. Table 2 shows that only 13 access terms or 19% of 70 schedule terms appear in the index. Further only 3 class numbers or 9% of 34 class numbers in the range are indexed while none of the fourteen Cutter numbers is indexed. Only ranges of specific numbers are indexed in this sample as Table 2 demonstrates. General form divisions, geographical divisions, and chronological subdivisions represented in Table 2 are not indexed at all for this range of numbers. It is most interesting that only the Douai version and the Challoner revision of the Douai version are indexed. Two of the access terms have inadequate structure and need to be rotated. The number of schedule terms appearing in identical form in the index is 2. This is 3% of the total schedule terms (70).

TABLE 2 — SUMMARY ANALYSIS OF BS 125-198

	Access Terms	Schedule Terms	Class Nos.	Class Nos. Indexed	Cutter Nos.	Cutter Nos. Indexed
Total	13	70	34	3	14	0
Specific Class Numbers	0	48	19	0	10	0
Specific Ranges of Class Numbers	3	22	15	3	4	0
General Ranges of Class Numbers	2	0	—	—	—	—
General References	2	0	—	—	—	—
Specific Cross References	2	0	—	—	—	—
Inappropriate References	4	0	—	—	—	—
General Form Divisions	0	16	6	0	9	0
Geographical Divisions	0	0	0	0	0	0
Chronological Subdivisions	0	0	0	0	0	0
Specific Subject Subdivisions	13	54	28	3	5	0

C: Auxiliary Sciences of History

CN 1-340 is representative of the diverse material included in this schedule as this range of numbers contains both general and specific headings for epigraphy. Sixteen access terms or 22% of 72 schedule terms are indexed in this range. Further from Table 3 only 6 class numbers or 23% of 26 class numbers in this range of numbers are indexed and one Cutter number of the three Cutter numbers is indexed. Once again a comparison of specific numbers and specific ranges of numbers in Table 3 shows that specific ranges of numbers are used with more frequency in the index than in the schedule. The subdivisions as demonstrated in Table 3 do not show any highly significant results other than the tendancy for specific subjects to be indexed more completely than the other forms of subdivision. Only one access term appears to need rotation. The number of schedule terms appearing in identical form in the index is 2. This is 3% of the total schedule terms (72) in this range.

TABLE 3 — SUMMARY ANALYSIS OF CN 1-340

	Access Terms	Schedule Terms	Class Nos.	Class Nos. Indexed	Cutter Nos.	Cutter Nos. Indexed
Total	16	72	26	6	3	1
Specific Class Numbers	2	59	26	2	3	1
Specific Ranges of Class Numbers	8	0	0	4	0	0
General Ranges of Class Numbers	1	0	—	—	—	—
General References	1	0	—	—	—	—
Specific Cross References	4	13	—	—	—	—
Inappropriate References	0	0	—	—	—	—
General Form Divisions	0	29	15	2	0	0
Geographical Divisions	3	9	2	0	2	0
Chronological Subdivisions	1	5	2	2	0	0
Specific Subject Subdivisions	12	29	7	2	1	1

D: General and Old World History

The complete range of numbers for this history of an individual country is chosen as the best representative sample for this schedule. DS 901-935 for the history of Korea is the range selected. As may be noted in Table 4, 46 access terms or 43% of 108 schedule terms are indexed in this range of numbers. However, only 13 class numbers or 27% of 49 class numbers are indexed. Five Cutter numbers or 31% of 16 Cutter numbers are indexed. Again from an examination of Table 4 it may be seen that ranges of numbers appear in the index to cover specific headings in the schedules. It is also noteworthy that this particular schedule has a more complete use of general references than the other schedules. All the access terms in this sample appear to have an adequate syntactical structure but some of the general references are very complex with inconsistencies. The number of schedule terms appearing in identical form in the index is 13. This is 12% of the total schedule terms (108).

TABLE 4 — SUMMARY ANALYSIS OF DS 901-935

	Access Terms	Schedule Terms	Class Nos.	Class Nos. Indexed	Cutter Nos.	Cutter Nos. Indexed
Total	46	108	49	13	16	5
Specific Class Numbers	13	108	49	11	9	5
Specific Ranges of Class Numbers	8	0	0	2	7	0
General Ranges of Class Numbers	0	0	—	—	—	—
General References	23	0	—	—	—	—
Specific Cross References	1	0	—	—	—	—
Inappropriate References	1	0	—	—	—	—
General Form Divisions	13	42	18	0	7	0
Geographical Divisions	13	14	5	4	6	4
Chronological Subdivisions	4	9	4	3	0	0
Specific Subject Subdivisions	16	43	22	6	3	1

E-F: American History

    The range of numbers for the history of the state of Colorado, F 771-785. is used as representative of this double class schedule. Table 5 shows that 69 access terms or 39% of 179 schedule terms are indexed in this range. Five class numbers or 25% of 20 class numbers are indexed. Table 5 shows that 27 Cutter numbers or 29% of 93 Cutter numbers are indexed. It is interesting that cities, rivers, and other geographical regions are indexed but that counties which are listed in the same list of Cutter numbers are not. There appears to be nothing unnatural in the comparison of specific numbers and specific ranges of numbers in Table 5. Again as in class D, the general references appear in this sample to be used more often than in the other schedules. The syntactical structure of access terms is all generally adequate. Forty-one schedule terms appear in identical graphemic form in the index. This is 23% of the total schedule terms (179).

TABLE 5 — SUMMARY ANALYSIS OF F 771-785

	Access Terms	Schedule Terms	Class Nos.	Class Nos. Indexed	Cutter Nos.	Cutter Nos. Indexed
Total	69	179	20	5	93	27
Specific Class Numbers	46	167	19	4	92	27
Specific Ranges of Class Numbers	1	1	1	1	1	0
General Ranges of Class Numbers	0	0	—	—	—	—
General References	14	0	—	—	—	—
Specific Cross References	5	11	—	—	—	—
Inappropriate References	3	0	—	—	—	—
General Form Divisions	14	28	12	0	1	0
Geographical Divisions	47	133	3	3	91	27
Chronological Subdivisions	0	4	3	0	0	0
Specific Subject Subdivisions	8	14	2	2	1	0

G: Geography, Anthropology, Folklore, Manners and Customs, Recreation
The folklore of mythical animals, plants, and minerals appears to be representative of the typical material of this diverse schedule. This range of numbers is GR 820-940. The indexing of this range of numbers appears to be far fuller than any sample previously considered. Table 6 shows that 43 access terms or 88% of 49 schedule terms are indexed. Coincidentally 14 class numbers or 88% of 16 class numbers are indexed while the eight Cutter numbers are fully indexed. Once again in this sample as in many of the previous ones, the specific ranges of numbers are used to index specific numbers in the schedule. As there are no subdivisions in this sample that are not specific subject subdivisons, the analysis of this section on specific subject subdivisions is the same as the total subdivision analysis for this sample. Three access terms have inadequate structure and need to be rotated. The identity figure for this sample is 45% as 22 schedule terms appear in identical graphemic form in the index.

TABLE 6 — SUMMARY ANALYSIS OF GR 820-940

	Access Terms	Schedule Terms	Class Nos.	Class Nos. Indexed	Cutter Nos.	Cutter Nos. Indexed
Total	43	49	16	14	8	8
Specific Class Numbers	29	44	16	10	8	8
Specific Ranges of Class Numbers	10	0	0	4	—	—
General Ranges of Class Numbers	0	0	—	—	—	—
General References	0	0	—	—	—	—
Specific Cross References	4	5	—	—	—	—
Inappropriate References	0	0	—	—	—	—
General Form Divisions	0	0	0	0	0	0
Geographical Divisions	0	0	0	0	0	0
Chronological Subdivisions	0	0	0	0	0	0
Specific Subject Subdivisions	43	49	16	14	8	8

H: Social Sciences

A portion of the complete subclass of numbers for communism is selected as representative of this schedule. This portion is HX 651-999. It may be observed in Table 7 that 24 access terms or 52% of 46 schedule terms are indexed. Eleven class numbers of 73% of 15 class numbers are indexed. Two of the three Cutter numbers are indexed. In this sample also it may be observed that specific ranges of numbers are used with more frequency in the index than in the schedule. While more specific subjects are indexed than any other subdivisions, it is interesting that this sample shows a fair percentage of general references. Six access terms need rotation because of their syntactical structure. The number of schedule terms appearing in identical graphemic form in the index is 12. This is 38% of the total schedule terms (46).

TABLE 7 — SUMMARY ANALYSIS OF HX 651-999

	Access Terms	Schedule Terms	Class Nos.	Class Nos. Indexed	Cutter Nos.	Cutter Nos. Indexed
Total	24	46	15	11	3	2
Specific Class Numbers	9	38	13	5	3	2
Specific Ranges of Class Numbers	8	2	2	6	–	–
General Ranges of Class Numbers	2	1	–	–	–	–
General References	1	0	–	–	–	–
Specific Cross References	4	5	–	–	–	–
Inappropriate References	0	0	–	–	–	–
General Form Divisions	6	18	10	6	0	0
Geographical Divisions	1	0	0	0	1	0
Chronological Subdivisions	0	1	1	0	0	0
Specific Subject Subdivisions	17	27	4	5	2	2

J: Political Science

JK 2071-2391, the range of numbers in this schedule for the electoral system and political parties, is chosen as representative of the type of material in Class J: Political Science. Table 8 shows that 40 access terms or 30% of 132 schedule terms are indexed. Twenty-four class numbers of 46% of 52 class numbers are indexed. The four Cutter numbers in this sample are not indexed. Table 8 shows that there are twice as many specific ranges of numbers in the index as there are in the schedule. Also it is noteworthy that only 9 specific access terms or 8% of the 111 specific schedule terms are indexed. The subdivisions as represented in Table 8 show no significant factors for analysis. All of the access terms have adequate syntactical structure. The number of schedule terms appearing in identical graphemic form in the index is 4. This is 3% of the total schedule terms (132).

TABLE 8 — SUMMARY ANALYSIS OF JK 2071-2391

	Access Terms	Schedule Terms	Class Nos.	Class Nos. Indexed	Cutter Nos.	Cutter Nos. Indexed
Total	40	132	52	24	4	0
Specific Class Numbers	9	111	44	17	2	0
Specific Ranges of Class Numbers	16	8	8	7	2	0
General Ranges of Class Numbers	6	6	—	—	—	—
General References	4	0	—	—	—	—
Specific Cross References	0	7	—	—	—	—
Inappropriate References	5	0	—	—	—	—
General Form Divisions	1	30	13	5	2	0
Geographical Divisions	16	5	3	1	1	0
Chronological Subdivisions	0	3	3	0	0	0
Specific Subject Subdivisions	23	94	33	18	1	0

L: Education

LB 2824-2853 was chosen as a typical page in class L after an examination of the schedule. This choice was necessary as no repetitive pattern could be discerned in this schedule. Forty-two access terms or 52% of 81 schedule terms are indexed in this sample. Table 9 shows that 14 class numbers or 64% of 22 class numbers are indexed. Only one Cutter number appears on this page of class L and it is not indexed. Table 9 shows that specific ranges in the index are used again for specific headings in the schedule. The specific subjects in Table 9 are the only subdivisions indexed in this example. There are three access terms which should be rotated to improve the indexing of syntactical elements. An additional three access terms need to have subdivision rotation and one access term introduces a nonexistent class number, "LB 2841". There are seven schedule terms appearing in identical graphemic form in the index. This is 9% of the total schedule terms (81).

TABLE 9 — SUMMARY ANALYSIS OF LB 2824-2853

	Access Terms	Schedule Terms	Class Nos.	Class Nos. Indexed	Cutter Nos.	Cutter Nos. Indexed
Total	42	81	22	14	1	0
Specific Class Numbers	19	66	22	12	1	0
Specific Ranges of Class Numbers	8	0	0	2	—	—
General Ranges of Class Numbers	7	1	—	—	—	—
General References	0	0	—	—	—	—
Specific Cross References	7	14	—	—	—	—
Inappropriate References	1	0	—	—	—	—
General Form Divisions	0	9	5	0	0	0
Geographical Divisions	0	6	6	0	0	0
Chronological Subdivisions	0	0	0	0	0	0
Specific Subject Subdivisions	42	66	11	14	1	0

M: Music and Books on Music

Orchestral music, M 992-1019, is selected as a representative sample of class M. As may be observed in Table 10, there are 39 access terms or 46% of 84 schedule terms that are indexed. It is most interesting that all 19 class numbers are indexed. There are no Cutter numbers used in this sample. There are no other significant factors in Table 10 for analysis. The syntactical structure of all of the access terms is adequate although the subdivisions of these terms are difficult to handle. The number of schedule terms appearing in identical graphemic form in the index is 7. This is 8% of the total schedule terms (84).

TABLE 10 — SUMMARY ANALYSIS OF M 992-1019

	Access Terms	Schedule Terms	Class Nos.	Class Nos. Indexed	Cutter Nos.	Cutter Nos. Indexed
Total	39	84	19	19	0	0
Specific Class Numbers	26	77	17	18	0	0
Specific Ranges of Class Numbers	1	2[a]	2	1	—	—
General Ranges of Class Numbers	1	1[a]	—	—	—	—
General References	6	0	—	—	—	—
Specific Cross References	5	4[a]	—	—	—	—
Inappropriate References	0	0	—	—	—	—
General Form Divisions	0	0	0	0	0	0
Geographical Divisions	0	0	0	0	0	0
Chronological Subdivisions	0	0	0	0	0	0
Specific Subject Subdivisions	39	77	19	19	0	0

[a] None of these terms are included in the subdivision analysis.

N: Fine Arts

NA 6800-7020, buildings for recreation, appears to be a representative range of numbers in class N. Table 11 shows that 22 access terms or 51% of the 43 schedule terms are indexed in this sample. Eleven class numbers or 65% of the 17 class numbers are indexed while none of the four Cutter numbers in this range is indexed. Again Table 11 shows that specific ranges of numbers in the index are used for specific headings in the schedule. Also once again it may be observed that only specific subjects are indexed. Only two access terms need to be rotated. Eight schedule terms appear in identical graphemic form in the index. This is 19% of the total schedule terms (43).

TABLE 11 — SUMMARY ANALYSIS OF NA 6800-7020

	Access Terms	Schedule Terms	Class Nos.	Class Nos. Indexed	Cutter Nos.	Cutter Nos. Indexed
Total	22	43	17	11	4	0
Specific Class Numbers	13	33	17	10	3	0
Specific Ranges of Class Numbers	3	0	0	1	1	0
General Ranges of Class Numbers	0	0	—	—	—	—
General References	0	0	—	—	—	—
Specific Cross References	3	10	—	—	—	—
Inappropriate References	3	0	—	—	—	—
General Form Divisions	0	2	1	0	0	0
Geographical Divisions	0	7	3	—	2	0
Chronological Subdivisions	0	2	2	—	0	0
Specific Subject Subdivisions	22	32	11	11	2	0

P-PA: Philology, Linguistics, Classical Philology, Classical Literature

The range of numbers, PA 4447.T5-4448.D45, including both names of classical authors and classical works, appears to be a typical page of the major section of this schedule. Although this schedule, unlike most of the subclasses of Class P, does have an index, none of the 57 schedule terms or the two class numbers or the 18 Cutter numbers is indexed. Because this characteristic appears to be typical of this particular index to this particular schedule the sample is retained and considered to be representative.

TABLE 12 — SUMMARY ANALYSIS OF PA 4447.T5-4448.D45

	Access Terms	Schedule Terms	Class Nos.	Class Nos. Indexed	Cutter Nos.	Cutter Nos. Indexed
Total	0	57	2	0	18	0
Specific Class Numbers	0	53	2	0	18	0
Specific Ranges of Class Numbers	—	—	—	—	—	—
General Ranges of Class Numbers	—	—	—	—	—	—
General References	—	—	—	—	—	—
Specific Cross References	0	4	—	—	—	—
Inappropriate References	(2)	0	—	—	—	—
General Form Divisions	0	3	0	0	0	0
Geographical Divisions	0	0	0	0	0	0
Chronological Subdivisions	0	0	0	0	0	0
Specific Subject Subdivisions	0	54	2	0	18	0

PB-PH: Modern European Languages

PG, in part: Russian Literature

PJ-PM: Languages and Literatures of Asia, Africa, Oceania, America, Mixed Languaged, Artificial Languages

There are no indexes to these three schedules.

PN, PR, PS, PZ: Literature (General), English and American Literature, Fiction in English, Juvenile Literature

The justification for choosing the two sections of subclass PR dealing with Anglo-Saxon literature has already been stated in Chapter 2, page 39. As Table 13 shows, 34 access terms or 25% of 135 schedule terms are indexed. Seventeen class numbers or 32% of 54 class numbers are indexed and two of eight Cutter numbers are indexed. The apparently consistent pattern of having a range of numbers in the index cover specific headings in the schedule appears once again. It may also be noteworthy that only 12 specific access terms or 9% of 130 specific schedule terms are indexed. Also once again only specific subjects were indexed in this sample although all other subdivisions were present as may be observed in Table 13. The syntactical structure of the access terms is adequate although once again the subdivisions create serious problems in the structure. The number of schedule terms appearing in identical graphemic form in the index is 7, or 5% of the 135 schedule terms.

TABLE 13 — SUMMARY ANALYSIS OF PR (Anglo-Saxon)

	Access Terms	Schedule Terms	Class Nos.	Class Nos. Indexed	Cutter Nos.	Cutter Nos. Indexed
Total	34	135	54	17	8	2
Specific Class Numbers	12	130	54	9	8	2
Specific Ranges of Class Numbers	9	0	0	8	0	0
General Ranges of Class Numbers	0	0	—	—	—	—
General References	3	0	—	—	—	—
Specific Cross References	1	5	—	—	—	—
Inappropriate References	9	0	—	—	—	—
General Form Divisions	0	16	10	0	0	0
Geographical Divisions	0	5	4	0	0	0
Chronological Subdivisions	0	4	4	0	0	0
Specific Subject Subdivisions	34	110	36	17	8	2

PQ, pt. 1: French Literature

PQ, pt. 2: Italian, Spanish, and Portuguese Literatures

PT, pt. 1: German Literature

PT, pt. 2: Dutch and Scandinavian Literatures

There are no indexes to these four schedules.

Q: Science

QP 166-348 was chosen as a typical page in class Q after an examination of the schedule. This choice was necessary as no repetitive pattern could be discerned in this schedule. Table 14 demonstrates that 58 access terms or 73% of the 80 schedule terms are indexed. Further 26 class numbers or 90% of 29 class numbers are indexed. There were no Cutter numbers involved in this sample. Although this index is obviously fuller than many others, it may be noted that the typical pattern of indexing specific headings in the schedule by using ranges of numbers in the index is present here. Table 14 shows that only 59% of the specific schedule terms are indexed and that only 73% of the specific class numbers are indexed. It may also be noted that the few general subdivisions included in this sample are not indexed. The indexing of specific subjects shows the highest level of percentage of schedule terms and class numbers that are indexed. Only one access term needs to be rotated. As might be expected the identity figure is much higher for this schedule than previously seen. The number of schedule appearing in identical graphemic form in the index is 26. This is 33% of the total schedule terms (80).

TABLE 14 — SUMMARY ANALYSIS OF QP 166-348

	Access Terms	Schedule Terms	Class Nos.	Class Nos. Indexed	Cutter Nos.	Cutter Nos. Indexed
Total	58	80	29	26	0	0
Specific Class Numbers	41	70	29	21	–	–
Specific Ranges of Class Numbers	7	0	0	5	–	–
General Ranges of Class Numbers	1	0	–	–	–	–
General References	0	0	–	–	–	–
Specific Cross References	5	10	–	–	--	–
Inappropriate References	4	0	–	–	–	–
General Form Divisions	0	4	2	0	0	0
Geographical Divisions	0	0	0	0	0	0
Chronological Subdivisons	0	0	0	0	0	0
Specific Subject Subdivisions	58	76	27	26	0	0

R: Medicine

RL 98-331 was chosen as a typical page in class R after an examination of the schedule showed no discernible repetitive pattern in the internal structure of the schedule. As may be observed in Table 15, 61 access terms or 80% of 76 schedule terms appear in the index. Twenty-eight class numbers or 93% of 30 class numbers are indexed. There are no Cutter numbers involved in this sample. Again the typical pattern of indexing specific headings in the schedule by using ranges of numbers in the index is present. Table 15 shows that only 45% of the specific access terms appear in the index and only 60% of the class numbers do. Further it may be noted that the specific subject subdivision section shows the highest percentqge with 100% of these class numbers indexed. The syntactical structure of the access terms is adequate. The number of schedule terms appearing in identical graphemic form in the index is 23. This is 30% of the total schedule terms (76).

TABLE 15 — SUMMARY ANALYSIS OF RL 98-331

	Access Terms	Schedule Terms	Class Nos.	Class Nos. Indexed	Cutter Nos.	Cutter Nos. Indexed
Total	61	76	30	28	0	0
Specific Class Numbers	29	65	30	18	—	—
Specific Ranges of Class Numbers	21	0	0	10	—	—
General Ranges of Class Numbers	1	0	—	—	—	—
General References	3	0	—	—	—	—
Specific Cross References	6	11	—	—	—	—
Inappropriate References	1	0	—	—	—	—
General Form Divisions	0	4	3	1	0	0
Geographical Divisions	0	0	0	0	0	0
Chronological Subdivisions	0	0	0	0	0	0
Specific Subject Subdivisions	61	72	27	27	0	0

S: Agriculture, Plant and Animal Industry, Fish Culture, and Fisheries, Hunting Sports

SF 361-415 is selected as a typical range of numbers in this schedule after an examination of the schedule showed no discernible repetitive pattern in the internal structure of the schedule. Table 16 shows that 45 access terms or 52% of 86 schedule terms appear in the index. Thirteen class numbers or 48% of 27 class numbers are indexed. Further 17 Cutter numbers or 90% of 19 Cutter numbers in this sample are indexed. This sample further demonstrates the pattern of indexing specific headings by ranges of numbers in the index. Also it may be noted that 21 general subdivisions are not indexed while 74% of the specific subdivisions are indexed. There are three access terms which should be rotated as a result of their syntactical structure. Further the structure of the access terms in this particular index includes many entries that tend to classified pockets in the alphabetical index: e.g., animal culture, forestry, horticulture, etc. The number of schedule terms appearing in identical graphemic form in the index is 20. This is 23% of the total schedule terms (86).

TABLE 16 — SUMMARY ANALYSIS OF SF 361-415

	Access Terms	Schedule Terms	Class Nos.	Class Nos. Indexed	Cutter Nos.	Cutter Nos. Indexed
Total	45	86	27	13	19	17
Specific Class Numbers	31	86	27	8	18	16
Specific Ranges of Class Numbers	11	0	0	5	1	1
General Ranges of Class Numbers	2	0	—	—	—	—
General References	0	0	—	—	—	—
Specific Cross References	0	0	—	—	—	—
Inappropriate References	1	0	—	—	—	—
General Form Divisions	0	21	9	0	0	0
Geographical Divisions	0	4	2	0	0	0
Chronological Subdivisions	0	0	0	0	0	0
Specific Subject Subdivisions	45	61	16	13	19	17

T: Technology

TP 936-978 is selected as a typical range of numbers in this schedule after an examination showed no discernible repetitive pattern in the internal structure of the schedule. As may be seen in Table 17, 42 access terms or 58% of 72 schedule terms appear in the index. Twenty or 69% of 29 class numbers are indexed and the one Cutter number in this sample is not indexed. Again the pattern of using ranges of numbers in the index for specific headings in the schedule may be noted. Also again the specific subject subdivisions are the most completely indexed subdivisions; however, in this case 25% of the general form divisions are indexed. Three access terms need rotation as a result of their syntactical structure and one access term appears in two inconsistent spellings. The number of access terms appearing in identical graphemic form in the index is 18. This is 25% of the total schedule terms (72).

TABLE 17 — SUMMARY ANALYSIS OF TP 936-978

	Access Terms	Schedule Terms	Class Nos.	Class Nos. Indexed	Cutter Nos.	Cutter Nos. Indexed
Total	42	72	29	20	1	0
Specific Class Numbers	20	62	29	15	1	0
Specific Ranges of Class Numbers	15	0	0	5	—	—
General Ranges of Class Numbers	2	0	—	—	—	—
General References	2	0	—	—	—	—
Specific Cross References	3	10	—	—	—	—
Inappropriate References	0	0	—	—	—	—
General Form Divisions	2	8	8	0	0	0
Geographical Divisions	0	0	0	0	0	0
Chronological Subdivisions	0	0	0	0	0	0
Specific Subject Subdivisions	40	64	21	20	1	0

U: Military Science

UF 470-565 on military artillery is used as a representative sample of this schedule on military science. This sample contains general subdivisions, geographical subdivisions and specific subdivisions. Table 18 shows that 25 access terms or 49% of 51 schedule terms appear in the index. Eight class numbers or 62% of 13 class numbers are indexed while two Cutter numbers or 18% of 11 Cutter numbers are indexed. The typical pattern of ranges of numbers in the index may be seen in this example also. This is also apparent in regard to geographical subdivisions as may be seen in Table 18. The syntactical structure of the access terms is adequate but there are seven individual terms that appear in the index for this range of numbers but not in the schedule. The number of schedule terms appearing in identical graphemic form in the index is 11. This is 22% of the total schedule terms (51).

TABLE 18 — SUMMARY ANALYSIS OF UF 470-565

	Access Terms	Schedule Terms	Class Nos.	Class Nos. Indexed	Cutter Nos.	Cutter Nos. Indexed
Total	25	51	13	8	11	2
Specific Class Numbers	6	43	6	3	10	2
Specific Ranges of Class Numbers	17	8	7	5	1	0
General Ranges of Class Numbers	2	0	—	—	—	—
General References	0	0	—	—	—	—
Specific Cross References	0	0	—	—	—	—
Inappropriate References	0	0	—	—	—	—
General Form Divisions	0	3	3	0	0	0
Geographical Divisions	5[b]	2	2	0	1	1
Chronological Subdivisions	0	0	0	0	0	0
Specific Subject Subdivisions	25[b]	46	8	8	10	1

[b] Five terms may be considered as both geographical and specific subject subdivisions.

V: Naval Science

VM 531-623 is selected as a typical range of numbers in this schedule after an examination showed no discernible repetitive pattern in the internal structure. Table 19 shows that 32 access terms or 50% of 64 schedule terms appear in the index. All 15 class numbers are indexed but none of the nine Cutter numbers are indexed. The consistent pattern of indexing specific numbers by ranges of numbers may be seen again in this sample. However, the general subdivisions appear to be indexed more fully than even the subject subdivisions in this range of numbers. Three access terms need to be rotated as a result of their syntactical structure. The number of schedule terms appearing in identical graphemic form in the index is 14. This is 22% of the total schedule terms (64).

TABLE 19 — SUMMARY ANALYSIS OF VM 531-623

	Access Terms	Schedule Terms	Class Nos.	Class Nos. Indexed	Cutter Nos.	Cutter Nos. Indexed
Total	32	64	15	15	9	0
Specific Class Numbers	18	52	13	13	6	0
Specific Ranges of Class Numbers	7	5	2	2	3	0
General Ranges of Class Numbers	3	0	−	−	−	−
General References	0	0	−	−	−	−
Specific Cross References	4	7	−	−	−	−
Inappropriate References	0	0	−	−	−	−
General Form Divisions	7	12	6	6	0	0
Geographical Divisions	2	2	2	2	0	0
Chronological Subdivisions	0	0	0	0	0	0
Specific Subject Subdivisions	23	50	7	7	9	0

Z: Bibliography and Library Science

The range of numbers, Z 2000-2049, is chosen because it contains general, geographical, chronological, and specific subdivisions of subject bibliography. As may be seen in Table 20, 25 access terms or 63% of 40 schedule terms appear in the index. Nine class numbers or 47% of 19 class numbers are indexed and all six Cutter numbers are indexed. The typical pattern of specific ranges of numbers in the index does not appear in this sample. Further the indexing of the general, geographical and specific subjects is different in this sample. Both geographical and general subdivisions are more fully indexed than the specifics. All the access terms have adequate syntactical structure but the general references are very complex and inconsistent. The number of schedule terms appearing in identical graphemic form is 4. This is 10% of the total schedule terms (40).

TABLE 20 — SUMMARY ANALYSIS OF Z 2000-2049

	Access Terms	Schedule Terms	Class Nos.	Class Nos. Indexed	Cutter Nos.	Cutter Nos. Indexed
Total	25	40	19	9	6	6
Specific Class Numbers	7	33	17	7	6	6
Specific Ranges of Class Numbers	4	5	2	2	0	0
General Ranges of Class Numbers	2	0	—	—	—	—
General References	8	0	—	—	—	—
Specific Cross References	4	2	—	—	—	—
Inappropriate References	0	0	—	—	—	—
General Form Divisions	7	12	7	0	0	0
Geographical Divisions	12	13	5	7	4	4
Chronological Subdivisions	0	2	1	0	0	0
Specific Subject Subdivisions	6	13	6	2	2	2

As may be observed in the total summary of the analysis tables (Table 21), 731 access terms or 44% of 1681 schedule terms appear in the indexes. Further, 281 class numbers or 51% of 555 class numbers are indexed while 84 or 35% of

242 Cutter numbers are indexed. Table 21 demonstrates the typical pattern of specific headings in the schedules being indexed by ranges of numbers rather than specific numbers. Further, Table 21 shows that specific subject subdivisions are more fully indexed than the other subdivisions. The identity figure of the total schedule terms appearing in the identical graphemic form in the index is 263. This is *15.6%* of the total of all schedule terms (1681). This summary shows the two patterns already noted appearing in consistent form. That is the analysis of specific numbers and specific ranges of numbers and the analysis of specific numbers and specific ranges of numbers and the analysis of specific subdivisions. Before beginning the section of this chapter on interpretation, it seems fair to say that the indexes in some cases tend to use specific ranges of numbers instead of specific numbers. This may lead one in the next section of this chapter to question the efficiency of indexing ranges of numbers rather than specific numbers. Also it may be stated that the indexes tend to be fuller in regard to indexing specific subject subdivisions than to indexing any other subdivisions. However it must be noted that some general form divisions, geographical divisions and chronological subdivisions are indexed.

TABLE 21 — SUMMARY ANALYSIS OF TABLES 1-20

	Access Terms	Schedule Terms	Class Nos.	Class Nos. Indexed	Cutter Nos.	Cutter Nos. Indexed
Total	731	1681	555	281	242	84
Specific Class Numbers	367	1493	512	199	219	81
Specific Ranges of Class Numbers	174	57[d]	43	82	23	3
General Ranges of Class Numbers	32	12[d]	—	—	—	—
General References	67	0	—	—	—	—
Specific Cross References	59	119[d]	—	—	—	—
Inappropriate References	32	0	—	—	—	—
General Form Divisions	65	316	154	32	28	0
Geographical Divisions	103[c]	250	67	20	112	36
Chronological Subdivisions	7	36	24	6	0	0
Specific Subject Subdivisions	561[c]	1072	310	223	102	48

[c]See Table 18, note b.

[d]See Table 20, note a.

INTERPRETATIONS AND CONCLUSIONS

In order to interpret the results of the analysis of the twenty samples of L. C. indexes, it seems necessary to integrate the individual results. Table 21 shows one form of integration. However, in attempting to test the consistencies of the indexes, it may be better to examine each aspect of the analysis in a relative manner. To do this the following seven tables are presented. These tables consist solely of the percentage of the aspect in the schedule to the aspect in the index. The actual figures contained in the previous tables are not included.

The wide variation of percentages in each column of Tables 22 and 23 may be interpreted as a factor of inconsistency among the indexes to the schedules. The percentage of schedule terms indexed and the specific subdivisions indexed show very parallel developments in Tables 22 and 23. This may be seen as the quality of the indexes to index more fully specific subjects than general, geographical or chronological subjects. One may also discern that the science and technology schedules are more fully indexed than the humanities and social sciences. In some cases, of course, individual disciplines in the social sciences appear to be very well indexed as in the case of Class G. The humanities appear to be the most poorly indexed. It must be noted that these two tables represent the percentage of schedule terms indexed by some form of access term. These are not identical graphemic matches.

Although Tables 24 and 25 show fairly wide variations of percentages in each, it does appear that there is fuller indexing of class numbers than schedule terms. In some cases it appears that the indexer was satisfied to have covered the class number in any fashion. Particularly, the specific subdivisions as represented by class numbers are more fully indexed than the other aspects. On the other hand, class numbers representing general, geographical and chronological subdivisions are often not indexed. One conclusion to be drawn from this interpretation is that specific subdivisions of class numbers are given greater indexing priority than other subdivisions of class numbers. This leads one to speculate that these indexes in general tend to be some sort of specific index and not a relative index.

Cutter numbers as represented in Tables 26 and 27 appear to present another peculiar set of inconsistencies. Although Cutter numbers included in the schedule are part of the classification number, many indexes simply do not index Cutter numbers. Other indexes index Cutter numbers either fully or in part. However, specific subdivisions as represented by Cutter numbers show very full indexing in general. Thus the conclusion drawn in the previous section on class numbers will also apply to Cutter numbers. Specific subdivisions of both class and Cutter numbers are given greater indexing priority than other subdivisions of class or Cutter numbers. It must be discerned that these figures on Cutter numbers are not entirely representative. In many cases all the Cutter numbers given in the schedule are indexed but these numbers may be introduced merely as examples in the schedules. The other Cutter numbers used by the Library of Congress may not be listed in the schedule or even the quarterly additions and changes and thus are not indexed. For instance under DS 916.5 for Korean

TABLE 22
PERCENTAGE OF SCHEDULE TERMS, SPECIFIC NUMBERS, AND SPECIFIC RANGES INDEXED IN INDIVIDUAL SCHECULES

Individual Schedules	Percentage of Class Numbers Indexed	Percentage of Specific Numbers Indexed	Percentage of Specific Ranges Indexed
Class G	88	66	n.a.
Class R	80	45	n.a.
Class Q	73	59	n.a.
Class Z	63	21	80
Class T	58	32	n.a.
Class H	52	24	400
Class L	52	29	n.a.
Class S	52	36	n.a.
Class N	51	39	n.a.
Class V	50	35	140
Class U	49	14	243
Class M	46	34	50
Class D	43	11	n.a.
Class E-F	39	28	100
Class B	35	25	400
Class J	30	08	200
Subclasses PN-PZ	25	09	n.a.
Class C	22	34	n.a.
Subclasses BL-BX	19	00	20
Subclasses P-PA	00	00	n.a.
All Schedules	44	25	365

biography and memoirs, Syngman Rhee is used as an example and given the Cutter number .R5. There are no other names of modern Korean leaders given in the schedule or the index although the entire range of numbers .A2-Z is reserved for this purpose.

TABLE 23
PERCENTAGE OF SPECIFIC SUBDIVISIONS, GENERAL FORM DIVISIONS, GEOGRAPHICAL DIVISIONS, AND CHRONOLOGICAL SUBDIVISIONS INDEXED IN INDIVIDUAL SCHEDULES

Individual Schedules	% of Specific Subdivisions Indexed	% of General Form Divisions Indexed	% of Geographic Divisions Indexed	% of Chronological Subdivisions Indexed
Class G	88	n.a.	n.a.	n.a.
Class R	85	00	n.a.	n.a.
Class B	83	25	08	33
Class Q	76	00	n.a.	n.a.
Class S	74	00	00	n.a.
Class N	69	00	00	00
Class L	64	00	00	n.a.
Class H	63	33	00	00
Class T	63	25	n.a.	n.a.
Class E-F	57	50	35	00
Class U	54	00	250	n.a.
Class M	51	n.a.	n.a.	n.a.
Class V	46	58	100	n.a.
Class Z	46	58	92	00
Class C	41	00	33	20
Class D	37	31	93	45
Subclasses PN-PZ	31	00	00	00
Class J	25	03	32	00
Subclasses BL-BX	24	00	n.a.	n.a.
Subclasses P-PA	00	00	n.a.	n.a.
All Schedules	52	21	41	20

TABLE 24
PERCENTAGE OF CLASS NUMBERS, SPECIFIC NUMBERS, AND SPECIFIC RANGES INDEXED IN INDIVIDUAL SCHEDULES

Individual Schedules	Percentage of Class Numbers Indexed	Percentage of Specific Numbers Indexed	Percentage of Specific Ranges Indexed
Class M	100	106	50
Class V	100	100	100
Class R	93	60	n.a.
Class Q	90	73	n.a.
Class G	88	63	n.a.
Class H	73	39	300
Class T	69	52	n.a.
Class N	65	59	n.a.
Class L	64	56	n.a.
Class U	62	50	72
Class S	48	30	n.a.
Class Z	47	41	100
Class J	46	39	88
Class B	37	25	225
Subclasses PN-PZ	32	17	n.a.
Class D	27	23	n.a.
Class E-F	25	21	100
Class C	23	08	n.a.
Subclasses BL-BX	00	00	20
Subclasses P-PA	00	00	00
All Schedules	51	39	191

TABLE 25
PERCENTAGE OF SPECIFIC SUBDIVISIONS, GENERAL FORM DIVISIONS, GEOGRAPHICAL DIVISIONS, AND CHRONOLOGICAL SUBDIVISIONS IN RELATION TO CLASS NUMBERS INDEXED IN INDIVIDUAL SCHEDULES

Individual Schedules	% of Specific Subdivisions Indexed	% of General Form Divisions Indexed	% of Geographic Divisions Indexed	% of Chronological Subdivisions Indexed
Class B	129	46	10	25
Class H	125	60	n.a.	n.a.
Class E-F	100	00	100	n.a.
Class M	100	n.a.	n.a.	n.a.
Class N	100	00	00	00
Class R	100	33	n.a.	n.a.
Class U	100	00	00	n.a.
Class V	100	100	100	n.a.
Class Q	96	00	n.a.	n.a.
Class T	95	00	n.a.	n.a.
Class G	88	n.a.	n.a.	n.a.
Class S	81	00	00	n.a.
Class L	79	00	00	n.a.
Class J	55	39	33	n.a.
Subclasses PN-PZ	47	00	00	n.a.
Class Z	33	00	140	00
Class C	29	13	00	100
Class D	27	00	80	75
Subclasses BL-BX	11	00	n.a.	n.a.
Subclasses P-PA	00	n.a.	n.a.	n.a.
All Schedules	71	21	30	25

TABLE 26
PERCENTAGE OF CUTTER NUMBERS, SPECIFIC NUMBERS, AND SPECIFIC RANGES INDEXED IN INDIVIDUAL SCHEDULES

Individual Schedules	Percentage of Class Numbers Indexed	Percentage of Specific Numbers Indexed	Percentage of Specific Ranges Indexed
Class G	100	100	n.a.
Class Z	100	100	n.a.
Class S	90	89	100
Class H	66	66	66
Class B	58	57	66
Class C	33	33	33
Class D	31	56	00
Subclasses PN-PZ	25	25	n.a.
Class U	18	20	00
Subclasses BL-BX	00	00	00
Class J	00	00	00
Class L	00	00	n.a.
Class N	00	00	00
Subclasses P-PA	00	00	n.a.
Class T	00	00	00
Class V	00	00	00
Class M	n.a.	n.a.	n.a.
Class Q	n.a.	n.a.	n.a.
Class R	n.a.	n.a.	n.a.
All Schedules	35	37	13

TABLE 27
PERCENTAGE OF SPECIFIC SUBDIVISIONS, GENERAL FORM DIVISIONS, GEOGRAPHICAL DIVISIONS, AND CHRONOLOGICAL SUBDIVISIONS IN RELATION TO CUTTER NUMBERS INDEXED IN INDIVIDUAL SCHEDULES

Individual Schedules	% of Specific Subdivisions Indexed	% of General Form Divisions Indexed	% of Geographic Divisions Indexed	% of Chronological Subdivisions Indexed
Class B	127	00	00	n.a.
Class C	100	n.a.	00	n.a.
Class G	100	n.a.	n.a.	n.a.
Class H	100	n.a.	n.a.	n.a.
Class Z	100	n.a.	100	n.a.
Class S	90	n.a.	n.a.	n.a.
Class D	33	00	66	n.a.
Subclasses PN-PZ	25	n.a.	n.a.	n.a.
Class E-F	23	00	30	n.a.
Class U	10	n.a.	100	n.a.
Class N	00	n.a.	00	n.a.
Subclasses P-PA	00	n.a.	n.a.	n.a.
Subclasses BL-BX	n.a.	00	n.a.	n.a.
Class J	n.a.	00	00	n.a.
Class L	n.a.	n.a.	n.a.	n.a.
Class M	n.a.	n.a.	n.a.	n.a.
Class Q	n.a.	n.a.	n.a.	n.a.
Class R	n.a.	n.a.	n.a.	n.a.
Class T	n.a.	n.a.	n.a.	n.a.
Class V	n.a.	n.a.	n.a.	n.a.
All Schedules	47	00	32	n.a.

TABLE 28
PERCENTAGE OF SCHEDULE TERMS APPEARING IN
IDENTICAL GRAPHEMIC FORM IN THE INDEX

Individual Schedules	Percentage
Class G	45
Class H	38
Class Q	33
Class R	30
Class T	25
Class E-F	23
Class S	23
Class U	22
Class V	22
Class N	19
Class B	14
Class D	12
Class Z	10
Class L	09
Class M	08
Subclasses PN-PZ	05
Subclasses BL-BX	03
Class C	03
Class J	03
Subclasses P-PA	00
All Schedules	16

Table 28 again shows the inconsistencies of the individual indexes. Graphemic identity ranges from nearly 50% to 3%. The humanities in particular show very little consistency in the use of vocabulary. This is, of course, not surprising as studies have shown that the area of the humanities contains many difficulties in vocabulary control. The only real surprise in these percentages is that Class G has the highest percentage of graphemic identity. Class G includes geography, anthropology, manners and customs, folklore, etc.

The previous seven tables have been used to demonstrate one form of interpretation of the results of the analysis of twnety individual samples. The conclusions drawn in this chapter are generalizations. There is really only one important conclusion: the indexes of the individual Library of Congress classification schedules are very inconsistent and are not in general representative of full indexes. The tendency of these indexes to favor specific subject subdivisions is a further weakness. The major lack of vocabulary control is still another weakness. The consistent pattern discerned in the analysis section that ranges of numbers in the index are used to index specific headings in the classification adds to frustration of the user. The classifier who must transfer from schedule to schedule and possibly from index to index will immediately experience the results of these inconsistencies and imperfections. The transfer from the index to Class G to the index to Class J is not a comfortable one if the samples used are representative. Class G has one of the best indexes according to the previous analysis and interpretation while Class J has an index with many schedule terms, class numbers, etc. that are not indexed. The individual accustomed to the general references of Class D or E-F will be confused by the lack of these general references in the sciences and by the complex general references in the humanities. These inconsistencies force the user to become familiar with each index as well as each schedule. In summation, the individual indexes to the schedules of the Library of Congress classification appear as a result of this analysis and interpretation to be both inconsistent and incomplete.

The implications of this chapter lead into the remaining hypotheses of this investigation. Obviously the present index terms do not represent a reversal of the schedule terms. The identity of schedule terms or classification headings to subject headings is the next phase to be investigated in testing the second hypothesis. The generation of a chain index in the third phase seeks another avenue of vocabulary control. This method attempts to develop identical and complete reversible indexing and classification.

CHAPTER IV

DEVELOPMENT OF THE ARGUMENT FOR ANALYSIS OF RELATIONSHIP BETWEEN L. C. SUBJECT HEADINGS AND L. C. CLASSIFICATION

INTRODUCTORY SUMMARY

The following 206 subject headings which were derived from three groups of samples are analysed from three different approaches. First the structure of the subject headings and the parallel classification and index headings are examined graphemically, morphologically and syntactically. It is hoped that this structural analysis will discern the parallel linguistic forms of these three approaches to subject analysis. Not only are the perfect matches or identities considered but also the variants of a perfect match are treated. The second analytical approach deals with the semantic parallels of the different headings. Pertinent headings are analysed for lexical meaning. Examples of contextual meaning are also isolated if possible. The third approach is an analysis of the classification numbers attached to the subject heading entry.

The structural analysis consists of three parts. These are graphemic analysis, morphologic analysis and syntactical analysis. The graphemic analysis consists of matching the shapes of the subject headings with the shapes of the classification and index headings. There are three possibilities which may result from graphemic analysis: match, partial match or no match. Match means that all of the symbols or graphemes making up a subject heading are present in the same order in the other heading being examined. Partial match means most of the graphemes are present but not in the same order or not in the same quantity. No match means that there is no parallel graphemic structure between the subject heading and the other heading. The morphologic and syntactical analysis follows directly from the graphemic analysis. A listing of partial matches begins this phase of the structural analysis. If the partial matches are represented symbolically, they may then be listed and tabulated. Those partial matches which appear to form paradigmatic classes are considered to be morphologic. If paradigmatic classes do not appear, the structure of the partial matches is considered to be syntactical. The use of any function word in the subject heading causes the heading to be considered as syntactical. It may be noted here that examples of repetitive syntactical structure occur very frequently in the subject heading list and only once in the sample covered.

Three groups of subject headings were analysed for graphemic structure. The first group contains forty-nine subject headings. The second group consists of eleven headings; and the third group contains one hundred and forty-six headings. The unevenness of these three groups results from the large number of subject headings contained in the syndetic structure of particular headings. The first group was generated from five random numbers and their appropriate headings. The first two headings generated only a total of five subject headings. The third heading 'Heraldry' generated thirty-four headings. The second group of four heading contained eleven headings and the last group (separated necessarily from the second group) contains all the subdivisions under the heading "Shakespeare". As these three groups total 206 subject headings, no further groups were generated. The author considers this sample to be large enough to test the methodology of this study.

	Classification	Index
Group 1 (49 SH)		
match	10	10
no match	21	17
partial match	23	27
Group 2 (11 SH)		
match	2	4
no match	4	2
partial match	6	3
Group 3 (146 SH)		
match	38	n.a.
no match	65	n.a.
partial match	50	n.a.

The index headings were not counted for group 3 as Shakespeare has only five index headings. These are:
    Shakespeare: PR 2750-3112.
        Authorship: PR 2937-2961.
        Biography: PR 2900-2936.
        Criticism: PR 2885-3088.
        Works: PR 2750-2875.
There is one additional entry in the Additions and Changes:
        Oxford, Edward De Vere, 17th earl of: PR 2947.
There are no entries for Bacon or anyone else involved in the Shakespeare authorship controversy.

	Classification	Index
TOTAL (206 SH)		
match	50	14 (of 60)
no match	65	19 (of 60)
partial match	79	30 (of 60)

In the first group of forty-nine headings 20% appear in identical shape in both the classification schedules and indexes. 43% do not appear at all in the classification schedules while 35% do not appear in the index. Partial matches make up the largest section of this group with 47% in the classification and 55% in the indexes. Similar patterns appear in groups two and three. However, it should be noted that in group three there are more 'no matches' than 'partial matches'. The total tally shows 25% of the classification and 23% of the index headings matching the subject headings. 35% of the classification headings do not match while 32% of the index headings do not match. 40% of the classification headings are partial matches and 50% of the index headings are partial matches. The graphemic analysis shows that about one-fourth of the sample of subject headings match perfectly with the classification and indexes. The size of the sample may preclude the possibility of drawing any further conclusions from these figures.

The second phase of the structural analysis considers the morphology and syntax of the same headings. Of the ten matches in the first sample, nine are direct matches of one word for one word in the classification. Similarly six matches in the index are direct matches of one mass noun for the same mass noun. The other matches in the first group each have a different pattern. These are 'word dash word', 'adjectival word', and 'word/word'. The term 'word' is used generally in these examples to mean a noun in mass form. The no matches of the first group have a very similar pattern. It appears then that the mass noun form is likely to occur in both groups more frequently than any other form. The partial matches show the greatest variety of forms. The form of a subject heading qualified by a gloss word in the index occurs seven times in the first group. The pattern of subject heading followed by a conjunctive function word and another word occurs twice in the classification headings and once in the index. All other forms in the first group occur only once. This is a total of twenty-nine different variants appearing only once in the sample. The partial matches show fifteen forms with additional contextual qualifiers and sixteen forms with some contextual qualifiers of the subject heading not present. The following charts show symbolically the varieties of form in the first sample. In these charts W means a noun in mass form, W_a an adjectival word, F a function word, F_c a conjunctive function word, f an article function word, SH a subject heading, and (sp) a spelling variation.

Chart 1 — Matches	Classification	Index
W	9	6
W–W	1	0
W_aW	0	1
W, W_a	0	1
W/W	0	1
$WFWF_cW$	0	1

	Classification	Index
Chart 2 — No match		
W	6	5
W (W)	1	1
W, W_a	1	0
W_a W	1	1
W F W	1	1
W F_c W	1	1
W_a W, W F f	1	1
W_a W W_a W F W, date—date	1	1
—W	3	3
—W F_c W	2	2
Chart 3 — Partial match		
SH (sp)	5	4
Partial matches with additional contextual qualification		
SH (W)	0	7
SH, W_a	0	1
SH F_c W	2	1
SH F W	0	1
SH, W F_c W	1	0
SH/F W F W	0	1
SH (W_a W)	1	0
W F_c SH	1	0
W F SH	1	1
W (SH . . .)	1	0
SH/ F W	0	1
SH/ W	0	1
W F f SH	1	0
SH, W F	0	1
Partial matches with some contextual qualification missing		
SH — ($\cdot Z_1$)	1	0
SH — ($\cdot Z_1$) (W F W)	0	1
SH —f —sh (W)	0	1
SH, —sh_a (F f W)	1	0
SH, —sh_a F W	0	1
-sh +W SH	1	0
—sh —f SH	1	1
SH (—sh)	1	1
SH — ($\cdot Z_1$) (—sh)	1	0
SH (—sh), W_a	0	1
SH —F —sh W, W, . . .	1	0

	Classification	Index
Partial matches with some contextual qualification missing (continued)		
SH —sh —F	0	1
SH (-Z_1) —W	1	1
SH —F —f —W	0	1
—W SH, W	1	0
(W, SH —f —sh)	1	0

Because of the great number of variations occuring in the first group and the apparent likelihood of this continuing as a seemingly endless list, the second and third groups were not analysed in this fashion. The only paradigmatic classes which appear to be present are the identities which require no transformation and the pattern of SH transformed to SH (W) in the index. The other classes may or may not be paradigmatic. The structural relationship between the subject headings and the classification headings or the index headings does not appear to be consistent in the transformations found in the sample.

The second approach used in this analysis is an attempt to isolate certain semantic features. Lexical meanings are isolated by using a dictionary meaning. This device allows synonyms and near synonyms to be discerned and classified. Further contextual meanings are isolated whenever possible and useful. This method shows that many subject headings apparently rely on the context of the subject heading list for their specific meaning. This context is often provided by a classification number, a scope note or syndetic devices. The area of semantics which the author has not yet been able to isolate deals with the conceptual meanings or the deep structure of the subject heading.

In the first group of samples, which were the only ones treated in this phase of analysis, there are twenty-five discernible semantic variants. All of these variants will be examined in the following section dealing with specific examples. The variants may be summarized as one instance of wrong contextual meaning, one instance of limited contextual meaning, one instance of expanded or redundant contextual meaning, eighteen instances of the contextual meaning contained in the classification number, two possible titles listed as subject headings, one instance of unclear conceptual meaning, and five classes of near synonyms involving twenty subject headings isolated by lexical meanings.

The last approach to analysis deals with the assigned classification numbers. The first sample includes four areas of inconsistency in these numbers. There is one instance of an apparently wrong class number, six number ranges that are too broad, four ranges that are too narrow, and five instances of unused appropriate class numbers. This is a total of sixteen classification inconsistencies in a sample of forty-nine headings or 37% of the headings in this group. In addition there are fourteen headings referring to more than one class number. These headings may apparently be considered as ambiguous in the sense of the classification system. Besides the first sample, the third sample dealing with Shakespeare shows many classificatory inconsistencies. Following the detailed discussion of the first sample, these Shakespeare headings will be rearranged in classified form and compared to the section of the classification dealing with Shakespeare. The only conclusion to be drawn at this point as a result of the summary of the classification number analysis is that the amount of inconsistency seems to be very great.

ANALYSIS OF THE DATA COLLECTED

This section presents all the headings included in the initial group. Each heading is analysed completely for structure, semantics and classification. The preceding summaries treated each operation separately. This analysis combines all the operations into a heading by heading approach. This technique is employed to show how few of the headings pass all the tests. At the end of this section a combined tally table will be given. Because of the detail of this technique only the first group will be considered.

The first random number under serial number 01400 in the Rand List is 40587. This means the first random heading is on page 1352 of the subject heading list in the third column and seven inches down the column. Hence the first heading in the first group is

United States Naval Expedition to Japan, 1852-1854 (DS 809)
    x   Japan Expedition of the American Squadron, 1852-1854
    xx   Japan—History

SH 1	CH 1	IH 1

United States Naval Expedition to Japan, 1852-1854 (DS 809)	—Asia
	  —Japan
	    —Description and travel
	      —1801-1900.
	DS 809
		Japan/Description and travel: DS 807-811

Graphemically this is a no match. W_a W W_a W F W, date—date is the morphological and syntactical structure. This formula may be transformed to W W F W and perhaps to W F W. It is very cumbersome in its present form. Semantically this heading represents in part what may be called a formal or proper name. Apparently this particular expedition is more commonly known as the Perry Expedition to Japan. This seems to be an instance of wrong contextual meaning if not wrong conceptual meaning. The class number is wrong as the xx references show. This heading appears to fail all four tests.

x 1 : 1	CH	IH
Japan Expedition of the American Squadron, 1852-1854		

Its only x reference is also a no match. Its structure is painfully close to the structure of the heading but seemingly grammatically imperfect. Can any other geographical name be logical substituted for Japan? *France Expedition of the American Squadron?

xx 1 : 1	CH	IH
Japan—History (DS 801-897)	DS 801-897 Japan —History (DS 851-889) —By period —19th century —Perry expedition to Japan, 1853-1854 (DS 881.8)	Japan/History/By period: DS 851-889

The xx reference for this heading leads to a much more generic heading. This heading matches graphemically in both the classification and index. Structurally this heading is 'word' dash 'word'. The index variation is minor. Both classification and meaning appear correct. The second random subject heading generated from number 29229 appears on page 974 nine inches down the first column.

Photogalvanography (TR 990)
xx   Photoengraving
Photomechanical processes

This heading gives the sort of results which the author had hoped to find.

SH 2	CH 2 TR 990	IH 2
Photogalvanography (TR 990)	Photogalvanography	Photogalvanography: TR 990

Both the classification and index headings match the subject heading. Morphologically the single mass noun is used consistently in all three sources. Both semantics and classification appear to be correct. This heading is a good example of direct consistency in subject analysis.

xx 2 : 1	CH TR 970	IH
Photoengraving (TR 970-77)	Photo-engraving (Relief processes)	Photo-engraving TR 970-77

The first xx reference must be scored as a partial match due to the spelling difference. Also the classification heading has additional contextual qualifications included in a gloss. The pattern of the structure is SH $(W_a W)$ for the change in the classification. The term in the schedule is apparently limited by its context.

This may also be seen in the variation in the class numbers. The subject heading appears to have too broad a range of class numbers. In both cases the index heading graphemically matches the subject heading but not the classification heading.

xx 2 : 2	CH	IH
	TR 925-99	
Photomechanical	Photo-mechanical	Photomechanical
processes	processes	processes
(TR 925-997)		TR 925-99

The last heading in this group shows a graphemic match with the index heading but not the classification heading. Structurally this is another case of different spelling. The meanings of the three terms appear to be the same. However, for some reason the subject heading classification number range is two numbers shorter than the classification schedule and index.

The third random number, 17594, directed the author to page 586 four inches down the second column. This leads to the subject heading 'Heraldry'. This heading has twenty-four sa references, five x references and sixteen xx references. There are also three subdivisions listed. Ten of the xx references also occur as sa references so that there are only thirty-four total to deal with as well as the five x references. The depth of this syndetic structure although initially distressing to the author proves to be most useful. It is in this sample that five classes of near synonyms are isolated. Also there are fourteen instances of contextual meaning contained in the classification.

SH 3	CH 3	IH 3
	CR	
Heraldry	Heraldry	Heraldry: CR
(National, CR;		
National: theory,	—Political theory	Heraldry, National/
JC 345)	—Symbolism, emblems	Theory: JC 345
	of the state: Arms,	Practice: CR
	Flag, Seal, etc.	
	—General works.	
	Theory.	
	JC 345	

The parent heading of this large family is checked in two different schedules as two different class numbers are given. In CR there is a graphemic match in both the schedules and the index. Its structure is a consistent single mass noun. Semantically this term is defined as

> The art or science of a herald; now esp. the art or science of blazoning armorial bearings, of tracing and recording pedigrees, and of deciding questions of precedence.[1]

The lexical meaning for this term may be used to demonstrate the first class of near synonyms. This includes blazonry, pedigrees, and precedence. Two of those terms appear as x references to heraldry which seems to acknowledge the near synonymity of the three lexical senses. Precedence, however, is itself a subject heading listed in heraldry's sa references. The class number CR for the entire subclass devoted to heraldry is appropriate. In the second class number attached to heraldry there is no graphemic match in the classification and a partial match in that index. Its symbolized structure is SH, W_a. It should be noted that the qualification 'National' in the index may also be found in heraldry's class numbers but not with the heading itself. This is a good example of contextual meaning contained in the class number.

sa 3 : 1	CH 3 : 1	IH 3 : 1
Achievements (Heraldry)	−Heraldry	(Ø)
(CR 41.A)	−Special	
	−Special branches, charges, etc., A-Z.	

The first sa reference in this family is very interesting in this same sense. 'Achievements (Heraldry)' is the only Heraldry reference which used the gloss word 'Heraldry'. There is no graphemic match for this heading. Morphologically this is a W (W) for which there is not match in the classification or index. Lexically we may discover a second class of near synonyms. The heraldry sense of this word is

An escutcheon or ensign armorial, granted in memory of some achievement. (In this sense corrupted to hatchment.)[2]

Escutcheon and hatchment are also sa references.

sa 3 : 2	CH 3 : 2	IH 3 : 2
	CR 67-69	
Badges	Devices and badges	Badges (Heraldry):
(Heraldry, CR 67-69)	67 General works.	CR 67-69
	69 By country, A-Z.	

Badges is the second sa reference under heraldry. It appears as a partial match in both the classification and the index. The form of the partial match is different however. CH = W F_c SH; IH = SH (W). The lexical meaning of this term introduces class 3 of the classes of near synonyms. There are a total of ten members of this class. Badge is defined as

A distinctive device, emblem, or mark.[3]

Contextually the qualification that badges refers specifically to heraldic badges is contained in the classification gloss and not in the subject heading gloss.

sa 3 : 3	CH 3 : 3	IH 3 : 3
	CR 79	
Battle-cries	Battle cries. War cries.	Battle cries:
(Heraldry, CR 79)		CR 79

The third sa reference shows a spelling variation between the subject heading and the classification. Also its contextual meaning appears to be contained in the classification gloss. Certainly there can be battle cries in history, literature, etc.

sa 3 : 4	CH 3 : 4	IH 3 : 4
	CR 4501-6305	
Chivalry	Chivalry and knighthood	Chivalry:
(CR)	(Orders, decorations,	CR 4501-6305
	etc.)	

Chivalry appears as a match in the index and a partial match in the classification. The partial match is SH F$_c$ W. This heading may be seen a member of class four of heraldic near synonyms. The other member is 'Knights and knighthood'. Again the contextual meaning is found in the classification number. It may also be observed that the classification number is too broad. CR 4501-6305 would seem to be more appropriate than simply CR.

sa 3 : 5	CH 3 : 5	IH 3 : 5
Color in heraldry	(∅)	(∅)
(no CN)		

This heading is not found graphemically in the classification or index. Its structure is W F W. It appears that it might be a possible title used as a subject heading. It is an approach outside of the structural treatment of heraldry in the classification system. (In the following examples only different variations will be cited.)

sa 3 : 6	CH 3 : 6	IH 3 : 6
	CR 55-57	
Crests	Crests	Crests (Heraldry):
(CR 55-57)	55 General works.	CR 55-7
	57 By country, A-Z.	

Crests is a member of class 3 as its lexical meaning states that it is "A figure or device".[4] Devices is also a sa reference.

sa 3 : 7	CH 3 : 7	IH 3 : 7
	CR 4501-6305	
Decorations of honor	Chivalry and knighthood	Decorations
(CR 4501-6305;	(Orders, decorations,	(Heraldry):
Milirary, UB 430-435)	etc.)	CR 4501-6305

This is also a member of class 3 as decorations are defined as "A star, cross, medal or other badge conferred and worn as a mark of honour."[5]

It would also seem that the phrase 'of honor' is an instance of expanded or redundant contextual meaning.

sa 3 : 8	CH 3 : 8	IH 3 : 8
	CR 67-69	
Devices	Devices and badges	Devices (Heraldry):
(Heraldry, CR 67-69)	67 General works.	CR 67-69
	69 By country, A-Z.	
	[see CH 3 : 2]	

Devices also belongs to class 3. Its lexical meaning also shows another near synonym.

> An emblematic figure or design, esp. one borne by a particular person, etc., as a heraldic bearing, etc.: usually accompanied by a motto ME.; also, a motto or legend borne with or in place of such a design.[6]

Mottoes is also a sa reference under heraldry.

sa 3 : 9	CH 3 : 9	IH 3 : 9
Emblems	(∅)	(∅)
(Art, N 7740;		
Christianity, BV 150-		
155; Comparative		
religion, BL 603;		
Heraldry, CR;		
Literature, PN		
6349-6358)		

Emblems which is a no match in regard to heraldry is also a member of class 3 of near synonyms. One of its lexical senses states, "A figured object used symbolically, as a badge."[7] It may also be noted that the classification reference to the entire subclass CR is too broad. In fact the number of classification references to various sections of the classification system may be interpreted as ambiguous from a classificatory sense. Certainly one may say that this particular subject heading must bring together material separated by the classification; but the value of such an ambiguous assemblage is questionable.

sa 3 : 10	CH 3 : 10	IH 3 : 10
Emblems, National	[see CH 3]	Emblems of state:
(no CN)		JC 345

Morphologically the partial matches of this heading are 'Emblems of the state' and 'Emblems of state'. The first of these partial matches seems to be an acceptable transformation of the subject heading. In fact 'of the state' appears to be substitutable for 'National' without requiring the inversion in the subject heading. The second partial match from the index is questionable from a grammatical sense. The omission of the article does not seem correct. Further in a classification sense it appears that there is an unused appropriate class number for this heading. JC 345 could be used as a classification reference.

sa 3 : 11	CH 3 : 11 CR 91-93	IH 3 : 11
Escutcheons (CR 91-93)	Shields and supporters 91 General works. 93 By country, A-Z.	(Ø) Shields (Heraldry): CR 91-93 Supporters (Heraldry): CR 91-93.

Escutcheons which has already been cited as a member of class 2 has no graphemic match in the classification or index. It is defined as

> The shield or shield-shaped surface on which a coat of arms is depicted; also, the shield with the bearings; a representation of this. A hatchment.[8]

From this lexical description a closeness between classes 2 and 3 of near synonyms may be seen. The contextual meaning shows that this subject heading is being used as a synonym for the classification heading 'Shields and supporters'; however, neither of the other members of class 2 refers to CR 91-93. Thus lexically all members of class 2 are near synonyms but contextually they are not. This seems to show a weakness in the classification headings as well as the subject headings.

sa 3 : 12	CH 3 : 12 CR 345-347	IH 3 : 12
Flags *(Emblems of state, JC 345-7; Heraldry, CR 101- 115;* Merchant marine signaling, VK 385; Military science, U 360-365, UC 590-595; Naval science, V 300-305	Symbolism, emblems of the state: Arms, Flag, Seal, etc. CR 101-115 Flags, banners, and standards	Flag (Emblem of state): JC 345-347 _____ Flags/As emblems of government: JC 345-7 Heraldry: CR 101-15

This heading with six classificatory references (two of which are considered under heraldry) is apparently ambiguous and too generic. Further the contextual meanings given by the classificatory references appear to be too limited.

sa 3 : 13	CH 3 : 13 CS	IH 3 : 13
Genealogy (CS)	Genealogy	Genealogy: CS

94

This is the fourth subject heading in this sample to pass all four analytical tests. It is the name of an entire subclass, CS, in the classification schedules.

sa 3 : 14	CH 3 : 14	IH 3 : 14
Hatchments	—Heraldry	Hatchments
(no CN)	—Special	(Heraldry): CR 41
	—Special branches,	
	charges, etc., A-Z.	
	CR 41	
	[example incl. hatchments]	

Hatchments already listed as a member of class 2 is defined as "An escutcheon or ensign armorial; = ACHIEVEMENT."[9] Further there is an appropriate class number for hatchments that is not used.

sa 3 : 15	CH 3 : 15	IH 3 : 15
	CR 4480	
Insignia	Royalty. (Insignia.	Insignia of royalty:
(Jeweled, NK 7400-	Regalia, crown and	CR 4480
7419; Military, UC	coronets, etc.)	
530-535; Naval, VC		
345; *Royalty,*		
CR 4480; Secret		
societies, HS 159-160)		

Insignia is another apparent ambiguous heading with limited contextual meanings. It is a member of class 3 of near synonyms.

> Badges or distinguishing markes of office or honour; emblems of a nation, person, etc.[10]

sa 3 : 16	CH 3 : 16	IH 3 : 16
Knights and knighthood	Chivalry and knighthood	Knighthood:
(CR)	(Orders, decorations,	CR 4501-6305
	etc.)	
	CR 4501-6305	

Knights and knighthood appears to a near synonym of Chivalry and has a classificatory reference that is too broad.

sa 3 : 17	CH 3 : 17	IH 3 : 17
	CR 4701-4775	
Military religious orders	Military-religious orders	Military-religious orders/
(CR 4701-4775)		Heraldry: CR 4701-75
		Numismatics: CJ 1691-7
		Seals: CD 5545-51

This heading which contains another spelling variation has a limited contextual meaning in its classificatory reference. The index to Class C shows additional uses of this phrase under both Numismatics, CJ, and Seals, CD. It would seem that either this heading should be further qualified to incorporate these other senses or it must be interpreted as limited only to military religious orders in heraldry. The lack of references to Classes B, Philosophy and Religion, and U, Military Science, is also questionable.

sa 3 : 18	CH 3 : 18	IH 3 : 18
	CR 73-75	
Mottoes	Mottoes	Mottoes (Heraldry):
(PN 6309-6318;	73 General works.	CR 73-5
Heraldry, CR 73-75)		

Mottoes has already been listed as a member of class 3 but its lexical meaning shows that it is also related to class 2.

> 1. Orign., a word, sentence, or phrase, attached as a legend to an 'impresa' or emblematical design. Hence, more widely, a short sentence or phrase inscribed on some object, and expressing an appropriate reflection or sentiment; also, a proverbial or pithy maxim adopted by a person as his rule of conduct. b. spec. in Her. A significant word or sentence usually placed upon a scroll, occas. having some reference to the name or exploits of the bearer, to the charges upon the shield or to the crest, but more often expressing merely a pious aspiration or exalted sentiment.[11]

sa 3 : 19	CH 3 : 19	IH 3 : 19
Nobility	(∅)	Nobility (Heraldry):
(Political theory,	Titles of honor, rank,	CR 3499-4420
JC 411-417; Social	precedence, etc.	
classes, HT 647-650)	CR 3499-4420	

The index heading gives an unused appropriate class number for this seemingly ambiguous heading.

sa 3 : 20	CH 3 : 20	IH 3 : 20
	CR 4501-6305	
Orders of knighthood	Chivalry and knighthood	Orders of knighthood and
and chivalry	(Orders, decorations,	knighthood and
(CR 4501-6305)	etc.)	chivalry: CR 4651-6305
	—Orders, etc.	
	CR 4651-6305	

This heading which may be considered a member of class 5 of near synonyms along with the above listed Nobility and the following heading Peerage but it may also be interpreted lexically as a member of class 3 and graphemically as a member of class 4. Further it is closely related to Military Religious Orders. And finally it has the same classificatory reference as Decorations of Honor.

sa 3 : 21	CH 3 : 21	IH 3 : 21
Precedence	Order of precedence	Precedence, Order of,
(CR; JX 1678-9;	CR 3575	see Order of precedence
Diplomatic,	[also subdivision 8 in	Order of procedence [sic]
JX 4081)	Table I]	General: CR 3575
		By country: CR 3600-4420,
		Subdivision 8, Table I

Precedence has already been cited as a member of class 1. Further its classificatory reference is apparently too broad.

sa 3 : 22	CH 3 : 22	IH 3 : 22
	CD 5001-6471	
Seals (Numismatics)	Seals	Seals/
(CD 5001-6471;	—Theory. Method, etc.	General: CD 5001-6471
National, JC 345-7)	5037 Relation to heraldry.	Seals and heraldry: CD 5037
	5041 Relation to	Seals and numismatics:
	numismatics	CD 5041
	Symbolism, emblems of	Seals, National: JC 345
	the state: Arms, Flag,	
	Seal, etc.	
	JC 345-347	

The first classificatory reference for this heading is too broad. CD 5001-6471 refers to Seals in general not seals and numismatics. Apparently from the index headings there should be such headings as *Seals, *Seals (Heraldry) and Seals (Numismatics). Only the third heading exists in the subject heading list although there are the following headings: Seals (Animals), Seals (Christmas, etc.), and Seals (Law).

sa 3 : 23	CH 3 : 23	IH 3 : 23
	CR 3499-4420	
Titles of honor and	Titles of honor, rank,	Titles of nobility:
nobility	precedence, etc.	CR 3499-4420
(CR 3499-4420)		

This heading also belongs to the apparently ambiguous class 5. There appears to be no precision of meaning for such terms as nobility, honor, rank, precedence, etc. in either the subject heading list or the classification schedule.

sa 3 : 24	CH 3 : 24	IH 3 : 24
Visitations, Heraldic	—Genealogy	Visitations, Heraldic/
(CS 410-497)	—By country	Great Britain: CS 419
	—Great Britain	County: CS 437
	and England	
	CS 410-499	

Lexically this heading means "A periodic visit made to a district by heralds to examine and enrol arms and pedigrees."[12] The classificatory reference refers only to British heraldic visitations. The inversion of this heading does not seem necessary. *Visitations (Heraldry) or even *Visitations would seem to have the same lexical meaning.

> also subdivision Heraldry under subjects, e.g. Book industries and trade—Heraldry; Popes—Heraldry; also particular heraldic devices, e.g. Collar (in heraldry), Coq gaulois (Heraldic device), Eagle (in heraldry), Elephant (in heraldry), Fleur-de-lis

The above note separating the sa references from the x references demonstrates the use of Heraldry as a subdivision. Only a census of the list could demonstrate this use fully. Heraldry as a subdivision is not considered in this paper. The examples of particular heraldic devices are somewhat disconcerting. The gloss may be (in heraldry) or (heraldic device). The latter seems to be a wiser choice as it does not involve the function word 'in'. Further there is no apparent reason why there are some heraldic devices listed as sa references, e.g. Achievements and Hatchments, and other such as Collars, Eagles, Elephants, etc. are not. It may also be noted that the x reference Gryphons would seem to fit into this group.

x 3 : 1-5	CH 3 : 25-29	IH 3 : 25-29
Arms, Coats of	(∅)	Arms (Heraldry), see Heraldry
Blazonry	(∅)	(∅)
Coats of Arms	(∅)	(∅)
Gryphons	(∅)	(∅)
Pedigrees	(∅)	(∅)

Four of the five x references are quite appropriately members of classes of near synonyms. Blazonry and Pedigrees are members of class 1 and Arms, Coats of and Coats of Arms are members of class 3. There is no apparent reason why Gryphons is listed as a see reference to Heraldry. Lexically gryphon is listed as the supposedly dignified spelling of griffin.[13] As already mentioned Gryphons or Griffins would seem to fit more logically in the group of particular heraldic devices. Surely a fabulous animal having the head and wings of an eagle and the body and hind quarters of a lion is not meant to be synonymous with heraldry.

xx 3 : 1	CH 3 : 30	IH 3 : 30
	CC	
Archaeology	Archeology	Archeology: CC
(CC; Art, N; Indian		By country: D-F
and other American		
antiquities, E-F;		
National antiquities		
other than American,		
DA-DU; Prehistoric		
antiquities, GN; Social		
antiquities, manners,		
and customs: general,		
GT)		

This would be a match if the spelling variation did not exist.

xx 3 : 2	CH 3 : 31	IH 3 : 31
	CT	
Biography	Biography	Biography: CT
(CT)		

This is the fifth heading to pass all the analytical tests.

xx 3 : 3	CH	IH
Chivalry	[see CH 3 : 4]	[see IH 3 : 4]
xx 3 : 4	CH	IH
Crests	[see CH 3 : 6]	[see IH 3 : 6]
xx 3 : 5	CH	IH
Decorations of honor	[see CH 3 : 7]	[see IH 3 : 7]
xx 3 : 6	CH	IH
Devices	[see CH 3 : 8]	[see IH 3 : 8]
xx 3 : 7	CH	IH
Emblems, National	[see CH 3 : 10]	[see IH 3 : 10]
xx 3 : 8	CH	IH
Genealogy	[see CH 3 : 13]	[see IH 3 : 13]

The above six xx references have already been analysed as sa references.
The varieties of generic and specific meaning that they represent demonstrates
the obvious problems in the syndetic structure of the subject heading list.

xx 3 : 9	CH 3 : 32	IH 3 : 32
History	(∅)	(∅)
(D: History and In-		
ternational law, JX		
1253; History and liter-		
ature, PN 50; History		
and philosophy, B 61;		

History and political
science, JA 78; History
and sociology, HM 36)

Although there are six classificatory references for this heading, heraldry is not
listed.

xx 3 : 10	CH	IH
Knights and knighthood	[see CH 3 : 16]	[see IH 3 : 16]
xx 3 : 11	CH	IH
Nobility	[see CH 3 : 19]	[see IH 3 : 19]

These two xx references are also circular references.

xx 3 : 12	CH 3 : 33	IH 3 : 33
Peerage	Peerage (Baronage)	Peerage/Great Britain:
(HT 647; Gt. Brit.,	CS 421	CS 421-3
CS 421-3)		Other countries: CS 80-2209

Peerage is a member of class 5 along with the previously mentioned Nobility
and Titles of honor and nobility. Its classificatory reference is apparently too
narrow according to the index heading.

xx 3 : 13	CH	IH
Precedence	[see CH 3 : 21]	[see IH 3 : 21]

Precedence has already been covered as a sa reference.

xx 3 : 14	CH 3 : 24	IH 3 : 24
Signs and symbols	CR 29 Symbolism	Symbolism/In
(no CN)		heraldry: CR 29

This is the second heading under heraldry that would seem to be a possible
title used as a subject heading. The heraldry classification and index headings
are probably more appropriate for the following subject heading, Symbolism.

xx 3 : 15	CH 3 : 35	IH 3 : 35
Symbolism	CR 29 Symbolism	Symbolism/In
(Christian, BV 150-		heraldry: CR 29
165; Civilization, CB		
475; Comparative		
religion, BL 600-620;		
Occult sciences, BF		
1623.S9; Psychology,		
BF 458)		

Symbolism does have an unused class number in heraldry as stated above. The
contextual meaning given by the present classificatory references appears to be
limited.

xx 3 : 16	CH	IH
Titles of honor and	[see CH 3 : 23]	[see IH 3 : 23]
nobility		

This is the tenth circular reference under heraldry.

–3 : 1-3	CH	IH
–Law and legislation	(∅)	(∅)
–Poetry	(∅)	(∅)
–U. S.	(∅)	(∅)

These three subdivisions are all no matches. Apparently these must be examples of possible subdivisions as there is no other apparent reason for their presence under this subject heading.

From the analysis of the subject heading Heraldry at least four important concepts may be discerned. First the use of lexical meaning has isolated five classes of near synonyms. These are

Class 1	Class 2	Class 3	Class 4	Class 5
Heraldry	Achievements	Badges	Chivalry	Nobility
Precedence	(Heraldry)	Decorations	Knights and	Titles of honor
xBlazonry	Escutcheons	of honor	knighthood	and nobility
xPedigrees	Hatchments	Devices		
		Emblems		
		Emblems, National		
		Crests		
		Seals (Numismatics)		
		Mottoes		
		Flags		
		Insignia		
		Orders of knighthood		
		and chivalry		
		xArms, Coats of		
		xCoats of Arms		

Second there are at least sixteen instances of the contextual meaning of a subject heading being contained in the classificatory reference. Third the use of several classificatory references under a single subject heading may cause an ambiguous assemblage to result. Fourth the syndetic structure of a generic heading such as heraldry is somewhat inconsistent. There are cases of circular unequal headings. The examples of particular heraldic devices are inconsistent. And there is one completely ambiguous or perhaps irrelevant see reference (Gryphons).

The fourth random number generated a shorter but no less ambiguous subject heading, Native races.

Native races (Colonization, JV 305-317; Protection, HV 3176-7)
Here are entered works on the relations between the governing
authorities and the aboriginal inhabitants of colonial or other
areas.
sa Ethnology
Native labor
Race problems
also subdivision Government relations under Indians of North America and
under names of tribes, e.g. Dakota Indians–Government relations;

101

and subdivision Native races under names of continents, countries, etc., e.g. Africa—Native races; Africa, South—Native races; Angola—Native races

  x Aborigines
  xx Ethnology
  — Education
    See Education, Colonial
    —Law and legislation
      See Educational law and legislation, Colonial

SH 4	CH 4 JV 305-317	IH 4

Native races
 (Colonization, JV
 305-317; Protection,
 HV 3176-7)
	—Colonies and Coloniza-
	 tion
	  —Relations with the
	  native races
		Native races and coloniza-
		 tion: JV 305-17

	CH 4 (cont.)	IH 4 (cont.)

	—Social Pathology
	  —Protection, assist-
	  ance and relief
	  —Special classes. By
	  race or ethnic group
	 3176—General works.
	 3177—Local. Associations
	  and institutions. By
	  place, A-Z.
		Native races, Protection
		 of: HV 3176-7

There appears to be more contextual meaning in the classificatory reference than in the scope note.

sa 4 : 1	CH 4 : 1	IH 4 : 1
Ethnology (GN)	(∅) (∅) (∅)	(∅) (∅) (∅)

This term does not occur in either of the schedules referred to in the parent heading's classificatory references. Ethnology may be found in subclass GN in Class G but not in Classes J or H.

sa 4 : 2	CH 4 : 2	IH 4 : 2
Native labor (no CN)	(∅) (∅)	(∅) (∅)

This heading does not appear to fit into the classificatory areas of the parent heading. In fact, the precise meaning of this heading is not clear.

sa 4 : 3	CH 4 : 3 HT 1501-1595	IH 4 : 3
Race problems (HT 1501-1595)	Races [This range of numbers appears closer to SH 4 than HV 3176-7.]	Races: HT 1501-1600

This heading which completes the sa references is equally confusing semantically. Its classificatory reference appears to fit Native races more appropriately than Race problems. The three sa references and their parent heading do not seem to have a clear conceptual meaning or meanings.

x 4 : 1	CH 4 : 4	IH 4 : 4
Aborigines	(∅)	(∅)
	[see CH 4]	Aborigines: HV 3176-8

This see reference has an appropriate index heading.

xx 4 : 1	CH	IH
Ethnology	[see CH 4 : 2]	[see IH 4 : 2]

This is a circular reference already covered under sa references. Neither of the subdivisions are found in appropriate classificatory locations.

The last heading in the first group resulted from random number 30633.

Precious Blood, Relics of the (BT 465)
- x   Blood, Relics of the Precious
-       Jesus Christ—Precious Blood
- xx   Atonement
-       Blood (in religion, folk-lore, etc.)
-       Jesus Christ—Relics of the Passion

SH 5	CH 5	IH 5
	BT 465	
Precious Blood, Relics	Relics of the Passion,	Relics of Christ: BT 587
of the (BT 465)	Cross, etc.	Passion, Cross, etc.: BT 465

This heading is more specific than its classificatory reference. The contextual meaning for this heading must be supplied either by the classificatory reference or the syndetic structure as the heading itself does not indicate whose "precious blood." Also the inversion of this heading does not seem to be appropriate.

x 5 : 1	CH 5 : 1	IH 5 : 1
Blood, Relics of the	Relics of the Passion,	Blood/of Christ: BT 590.B5
Precious	Cross, etc.	Precious blood/Relics of:
	BT 465	BT 465
	Blood of Christ	
	BT 590.B5	

This x reference shows one possible permutation on the parent heading. Apparently the further permutation of the heading to normal natural language order is not deemed necessary.

x 5 : 2	CH 5 : 2	IH 5 : 2
Jesus Christ—Precious	[see CH 5 : 1]	Jesus Christ: BT 198-590
Blood		Blood of: BT 590.B5
		Relics: BT 465, (585)-587

Again this x reference is confusing semantically. Does this phrase refer to the blood, the relics of the blood, or symbolic use of blood? There are separate index headings for these different senses.

xx 5 : 1	CH 5 : 3	IH 5 : 3
Atonement	—Christology	Atonement/Christology:
(BT 264-5)	—Offices of Christ	BT 262-268
	—Priestly office	
	—Sacrifice.	
	Atonement.	
	Reconciliation.	
	Satisfaction.	
	BT 262-268	

Once again with this heading only from the classificatory reference do we know whose atonement is meant. It may also be noted that the classificatory range is too narrow in the reference.

xx 5 : 2	CH 5 : 4	IH 5 : 4
	BL 570	
Blood (in religion,	Sacrifice. Offerings. Vows. (Ø)	
folk-lore, etc.)		
(Comparative	BL 600	
religion, BL 570	Rites and ceremonies.	
BL 600; Folk-lore,	Ritual, cult, symbolism.	
GR 489)		

The contextual meanings that may be drawn from the classificatory references for this heading are in seemingly poor taste if accurate.

xx 5 : 3	CH 5 : 5	IH 5 : 5
Jesus Christ—Relics of	[see CH 5]	Jesus Christ; BT 198-590
the Passion (BT 465)		Relics: BT 465, (585)-587

One can only wonder why the form of this heading could not be used for the parent heading. *Jesus Christ—Relics of the Precious Blood.

The first sample group of forty-nine headings may be summarized in the following table. Only five headings or less than 10% pass all the tests. In order to pass a heading must be structurally a match in the subject heading list, the classification schedule and the index to that schedule. Second the heading must pass the semantic tests. It must not be a member of a class of near synonyms that could be interchanged. Its contextual meaning must appear in the heading and not in the classificatory references or the syndetic structure. Third, the heading must have the appropriate classificatory reference. The following list of five headings out of forty-nine pass all the tests:

JAPAN—HISTORY
PHOTOGALVANOGRAPHY
HERALDRY (in its first classificatory reference only)
GENEALOGY
BIOGRAPHY

	Structure	Semantics	Classification
SH 1	∅	∅	∅
x 1	∅	∅	na
xx 1	P	P	P
SH 2	P	P	P
xx 1	∅	∅	∅
xx 2	∅	P	∅
SH 3	P	P	P
	∅	P	∅
sa 1	∅	∅	P
sa 2	∅	∅	P
sa 3	∅	∅	P
sa 4	∅	∅	∅
sa 5	∅	∅	∅
sa 6	∅	∅	P
sa 7	∅	∅	P
sa 8	∅	∅	P
sa 9	∅	∅	∅
sa 10	∅	P	∅
sa 11	∅	∅	P
sa 12	∅	∅	P
sa 13	P	P	P
sa 14	∅	∅	∅
sa 15	∅	∅	P
sa 16	∅	∅	∅
sa 17	∅	∅	∅
sa 18	∅	∅	P
sa 19	∅	∅	∅
sa 20	∅	∅	P
sa 21	∅	∅	∅
sa 22	∅	∅	∅
sa 23	∅	∅	P
sa 24	∅	P	∅
x 1-5	∅	∅	na
xx 1	∅	P	P
xx 2	P	P	P
xx 3-8	already counted		
xx 9	∅	P	∅
xx 10-11	already counted		
xx 12	∅	∅	∅
xx 13	already counted		
xx 14	∅	∅	∅
xx 15	∅	P	∅
xx 16	already counted		

	Structure	Semantics	Classification
−1-3	∅	∅	∅
SH 4	∅	∅	∅
sa 1	∅	∅	∅
sa 2	∅	∅	∅
sa 3	∅	∅	∅
xx 1	already counted		
−1-2	∅	∅	∅
SH 5	∅	∅	∅
xx 1	∅	P	∅
xx 2	∅	∅	∅
xx 3	∅	P	P

In concluding this part of the section on the data collected the members of group 2 are simply listed.

Law, Primitive   (GN 493)
    sa   Ethnological jurisprudence
    xx   Ethnological jurisprudence
          Society, Primitive

Tepanecas   (F 1219)
    x   Tecpanecas
    xx   Indians of Mexico
          Nahuas

Croation peotry   (Collections, PG 1614; History, PG 1610)
    sa   Croation poetry in foreign countries

School buses
    xx   Motor buses
          School children—Transportation

Of these eleven headings only Tepanecas passes all the tests.

There are only four personal names in the L. C. subject heading list. The next random sample forced the author into the middle of one of these four, Shakespeare. There are nearly 145 subdivisions and sub-subdivisions under Shakespeare. Most of these have classificatory references to the section of subclass PR, English literature, for Shakespeare. The structural and semantic tests are not used on this heading and its family. Although the graphemic test was applied, the morphologic test was not as the form of these subdivisions is particular to individual authors. Further the semantic variations were not tabulated as all the subdivisions appear to be in the same general area of semantic meaning. Major semantic differences will, of course, be obvious from the classification test. This parent heading demonstrates the differences between subject headings and classification headings. By rearranging these subject headings into the order of their classificatory references, they may be compared with the classification schedules.

The most obvious inconsistencies are the use of multiple subdivisions referring to the same number or range of numbers in the classification, 15 unused appropriate classificatory references and the inconsistent use of sub-divisions under the two subdivisions "Knowledge" and "Characters". The

many cases of inconsistent use of terminology should also be apparent. As
most of these subdivisions have classificatory references one might assume that
a high degree of consistency with the classification terminology and treatment.
This is not the case with Shakespeare. Possibly subject headings could be
created from the classification headings by simply creating a chain index as the
following chapter demonstrates. For example PR 3078, syntax, could be
indexed as demonstrated in chapter two:

      SYNTAX: SHAKESPEARE, PR 3078
      GRAMMAR: SHAKESPEARE, PR 3075-3081
      LANGUAGE: CRITICISM: SHAKESPEARE, PR 3072-3088
      CRITICISM: SHAKESPEARE, PR 2965-3088
      Interpretation SHAKESPEARE, PR 2965-3088
      SHAKESPEARE, WILLIAM, PR 2750-3112

There would have to be summary cards under Shakespeare as well as individual
feature cards.

INTERPRETATIONS AND CONCLUSIONS

Of the 206 subject headings tested graphemically, about one-fourth
match perfectly with both the classification and index headings. 40% of the
classification headings are partial matches and 50% of the index headings are
partial matches. The morphological-syntactical analysis shows a single noun in
mass form to be the only recurring perfect match in the first group of 49 subject
headings. The partial matches of the first group form 31 different variants
with only two forms recurring. The only paradigmatic classes which appear to
be present are the identities which require no transformation and the pattern of
SH transformed to SH (W) in the index which occurs seven times in the partial
matches of the first group. In the first group there are 25 discernible semantic
variants. These variants may be summarized as one wrong contextual meaning,
one limited contextual meaning, one expanded or redundant contextual meaning, eighteen contextual meanings contained in the classificatory reference, two
possible titles used as subject headings, and five classes of near synonyms
isolated by lexical meanings. There are four different inconsistencies in the
classificatory references of the first group. There is one instance of an apparently
wrong class number, six number ranges that are too broad, four ranges that
are too narrow, and five instances of unused appropriate class numbers. The
Shakespeare example shows many subdivisions referring to the same number
or range of numbers, fifteen unused appropriate classificatory references and
an inconsistent use of sub-subdivisions. When the results of the structural,
semantic and classification tests are combined, only five headings or 10% of
the first group pass all the tests. In the second group of eleven headings only
one passes all the tests.

The size of the sample limits the interpretation to specific statements
about the sample and only general statements about the entire list. It appears
that the sample covered is only coincidentally related to the classification

system. One cannot positively state that the samples used are truly representative of the entire list but there is no reason to state that they are not. The sample clearly demonstrates cases of near synonyms, ambiguous headings and redundant headings. Further the existence of three vocabularies appears to be proved in the sample. There is the vocabulary of the classification schedules, a different vocabulary of the subject headings, and even a third vocabulary of the classification index.

Another major value of this chapter is the success of the methodology. It appears that the methodology will show several levels of inconsistency. These levels are structural on both graphemic and morphologic-syntactical approaches, semantic on both lexical and contextual approaches, and classificatory. The value of the additional tests beyond the graphemic matches may be proved by the 50% reduction of the perfect matches in the first group when the other tests are applied. The graphemic display of the Shakespeare sample shows the value of the classificatory test applied in isolation. Both ambiguous headings and redundant headings may be readily observed in this fashion. In addition cases of near synonyms may be predicted as well as isolating unused classificatory references.

The results of this chapter lead directly into the third hypothesis of this investigation. If the testing methods used in this chapter and the previous one demonstrate inconsistent use of vocabulary, can a chain index solve this problem? An experimental model of chain indexing could be developed from a parent heading such as Heraldry or Shakespeare. Such a model would have to follow strict structural and semantic rules to integrate the vocabularies of the chain index, the classification schedule, the classification index, and the subject headings into one vocabulary. This model could then allow the index to be the list of subject headings. Further this model would allow the classification schedules to be fully indexed. Inherent in the generation of this model would be the development of rules for chain indexing. These rules would then need to be applied to other examples.

[1] *The Oxford Universal Dictionary on Historical Principles.* Prepared by William Little, H. W. Fowler, J. Coulson. Revised and edited by C. T. Onions. (3d ed. rev.; Oxford: At the Clarendon Press, 1955), p. 892.

[2] *Ibid.,* p. 15.

[3] *Ibid.,* p. 136.

[4] *Ibid.,* p. 421.

[5] *Ibid.,* p. 465.

[6] *Ibid.,* p. 496.

[7] *Ibid.,* p. 597.

[8] *Ibid.,* p. 632.

[9] *Ibid.,* p. 871.

[10] *Ibid.,* p. 1015.

[11] *Ibid.,* p. 1288.

[12] *Ibid.,* pp. 2363-64.

[13] *Ibid.,* p. 831.

CHAPTER V

DEVELOPMENT OF THE ARGUMENT FOR THE EXPERIMENTAL MODEL OF CHAIN INDEXING L. C. CLASSIFICATION AND THE FORMULATION OF RULES

INTRODUCTION

The first statement of Ranganathan's concept of chain indexing appears in *Theory of Library Catalogue*[1] published in 1938. He says in a later work, *Classified Catalogue Code,* of these rules

> When the Rules of Chain Procedure were formulated for the first time in 1938 in *Theory* (RT 10), the rules were crude. For, practically every significant digit in the class number was given the right to claim a Class Index Entry of its own. For example, in the class number L183, the digit 3 gave the class index heading, "Ear, Medicine." The digit 8 also gave the class index heading "Head, Medicine." Again, the digit 1 too gave the class index heading "Regional Organ, Medicine." This was a ruthlessly mechanical way of deriving class index entries from the digits in class number. It lead to a plethora of class index entries. Some of these were irritating the mind vaguely. The Law of Parsimony protested. But there was no way of removing the irritation, till the Canon of Sought-Heading took shape. It ruled out as unsought the two headings "Head, Medicine," and "Regional Organ, Medicine." Similar weeding out of unsought headings was indicated in many classes. The Rules of Chain Procedure were themselves re-enunciated.[2]

In neither of these sources does Ranganathan present detailed rules for form and context.

Jack Mills in his 1955 article, "Chain Indexing and Classified Catalogue,"[3] offers eight basic principles or procedures for chain indexing.

Mills has amplified these principles in several other writings.[4] Additional statements of procedure may be found in Kennedy[5], Palmer and Wells[6], and in C. D. Batty's article in a forthcoming volume of the *Encyclopedia of Library and Information Science.*[7]

As most of these writings have a referential base in Mills' 1955 article, the eight basic procedures of that article should be carefully examined. Mills first two steps may be interpreted as preparatory steps. These steps are designed to analyse the classificatory hierarchy prior to generating the index.

1. Each subject receiving an entry in the classified file is
analysed as a series of steps of division from the main class
to the specific subject. In making this rough preliminary
statement of the hierarchy (which should never be omitted,
however skilled the cataloguer), the terms found in the
schedules of the scheme are used. For convenience of
reference, each step in the examples below is numbered.[8]

Mills provides individual examples of these principles. The following examples,
however, are provided by the investigator in hopes of clarifying later sections
of this chapter.

1.	P	Philology and literature
2.	PR	English literature
3.	PR 2199-3195	English renaissance (1500-1640)
4.	PR 2411-3195	The drama
5.	PR 2417-3195	Individual authors
6.	PR 2750-3112	Shakespeare, William
7.	PR 2965-3088	Criticism and interpretation
8.	PR 3072-3088	Language
9.	PR 3075-3081	Grammar
10.	PR 3078	Syntax

Mills second procedure is

2. If the classification scheme does not give sufficient detail,
further steps of division must be supplied by the cataloger.[9]

This may be demonstrated in the following manner. If the above examples
dealt with Shakespeare's syntactical use of immediate constituents, point 11
could be "Immediate constituents."

. . .

10.	PR 3078	Syntax
11.	PR 3078	Immediate constituents

This is the basic method of allowing the index to present closer classification
than the notation of the system does. It is often used in the *B.N.B.*[10]
These two steps show the great reliance of chain indexing on the classificatory
order and terminology of the classification system.

The third step of Mills' procedure begins generating or creating the
index terms.

3. Beginning with the *last* step of division, index entries are now
made for each significant step, adjusting the terms of classification
where necessary (e.g., replacing American terms by British
terms). As far as possible the style followed in the *B.N.B.*
should be consistently maintained, i.e., of plural nouns
separated by colons; this facilitates filing by avoiding the
clumsy succession of groups under a subject (form divisions,
period divisions, inverted phrases, etc.) which can be so
confusing in the Dictionary Catalogue.[11]

This step begins the basic analysis and development of the index terms. The hierarchy or classificatory order is reversed.

11.	PR 3078	Immediate constituents
10.	PR 3078	Syntax
9.	PR 3075-3081	Grammar
8.	PR 3072-3088	Language
7.	PR 2965-3088	Criticism and interpretation
6.	PR 2750-3112	Shakespeare, William
5.	PR 2417-3195	Individual authors
4.	PR 2411-3195	The drama
3.	PR 2199-3195	English renaissance (1500-1640)
2.	PR	English literature
1.	P	Philology and literature

The access terms or the first terms of the index terms are analysed for possible adjustment. Problems of British vs. American terminology must be considered. Both of these problems of vocabulary control are covered by Mills' seventh principle concerning synonyms. However in analyzing this step of initial links there is one basic problem for consideration. Should the terms be inverted from the order of natural language? Mills states, ". . . there is no need for inversion."[12] Scheerer says of inversion,

> Every cataloger who has questioned his student assistants
> knows that to invert or not to invert is in the realm of the
> psychologically incalculable and that the decision must be made
> upon an objective, not a mind-reading, basis. The guiding
> principles should be the grammatical structure of the concept
> and the essentials of card catalog communication.[13]

Mills will allow inversion, and this would include rotational inversion, only if ". . . the second term in a phrase is not covered by a superordinate link."[14] For instance in the above example entry 2 "English literature" could not be inverted because "Literature" is covered by a superordinate link, entry 1.

The fourth step may be called the weeding or discard step. Any links in the inverted hierarchical analysis that are not necessary for index terms are removed.

> 4. Steps are deemed to be not significant if they are (a) *false links:*
> (i) connecting symbols (such as the 09 in Dewey, which is usually
> merely a symbol indicating division by country), (ii) concepts
> which are virtually nameless (such as periods of time); (b)
> *unsought links*, i.e., the terms are not of a kind likely to be
> consulted by a user of the library.[15]

Unsought links are discarded in accordance with Ranganathan's previously mentioned Canon of Sought-Heading. Mills says further in this vein,

> Steps of division represented by words which are not likely
> to be sought by readers (e.g., Theory, Organization) are
> omitted, or are given a general reference (e.g., Dictionaries
> on special subjects, *see* subject, instead of, say, Dictionaries:

Chemistry 540.3). Period divisions usually come into this category of "unsought links" in the chain; but "Medieval" is often regarded as an exception. This example emphasizes that chain indexing does not dispense with the individual discretion of the indexer, or the need for him to be alive to the terms used by the readers.[16]

Coates also states in regard to unsought links,

> The Decimal Classification *notational* hierarchy may contain such verbal equivalents as "general", "special", "other", "miscellaneous", "divided like". Such terms have, of course, no name-value; they merely indicated the structure of the classification schedule, and should be omitted from the basic analysis.[17]

The application of this concept would probably remove entries 3 and 5 from the previous example. Entry 3, "English renaissance (1500-1640)" is a chronological division and entry 5 "Individual authors" appears to be an unsought link.

11.	PR 3078	Immediate constituents
10.	PR 3078	Syntax
9.	PR 3075-3081	Grammar
8.	PR 3072-3088	Language
7.	PR 2965-3088	Criticism and interpretation
6.	PR 2750-3112	Shakespeare, William
4.	PR 2411-3195	The drama
2.	PR	English literature
1.	P	Philology and literature

The application of this principle obviously requires a subjective judgment. As Derek Langridge states,

> Often the vague word is the leading term in natural language and it would certainly provide the most specific entry for a chain index. Perhaps we have created a vicious circle here. We do not use the words for entry, so the searcher is discouraged from this type of approach, so we brand them as unsought terms and do not use the words so . . . The moral is, not to base our principles too much on the way we *think* laymen use an index.[18]

In fact Miss Herrick notes a value for the use of the subdivision "general works" which may be applicable to chain indexing.

> The consistent use of the subdivision *general works* under every major subject area provides a sure guide to broad treatment suitable for the undergraduate writing a paper or for the specialist from another field who is intent on getting some basic material in a subject remote from his own activities.[19]

112

Whether or not this discard principle should be followed will be discussed later in this chapter.

Mills fifth step merely points out that all steps or links are indexed.

> 5. All significant steps are indexed automatically, whether or not the library possesses a book specifically on each of them.[20]

This means simply that "Grammar" is indexed even if we have only a book on Shakespeare's syntax and not specifically on his grammar in general.

Step six is perhaps the most important step in the chain indexing procedure. Obviously the individual index entries previously generated present some ambiguities. "Syntax" refers in our context to Shakespeare's use of syntax, not to syntax in general. This step may be called the contextual principle.

> 6. If necessary (and it usually is), the first word of the index entry (the *main heading*) must be qualified by superordinate terms from the hierarchy in order to show which aspect of the subject is meant, i.e., what its context is. These qualifying terms are called *sub-headings* and those are chosen which give the context as concisely as possible. They are taken from the chain in a strict order of increasing generalness.[21]

Mills further states,

> Since the purpose of the sub-heading is to place the main heading (the first word) in a *wider context,* it follows that it must always be a *more general term* than the main heading; that is why it is taken from the superordinate links and if there are more than one needed, they are given in the order of the chain, each one successively wider (i.e., taken from higher up in the hierarchy).[22]

If the links remaining after step 4 are qualified by the necessary superordinate terms in accordance with this step, the following example will result.

11. Immediate constituents: Syntax: Shakespeare, PR 3078
10. Syntax: Shakespeare, PR 3078
9. Grammar: Shakespeare, PR 3075-3081
8. Language: Criticism: Shakespeare, PR 3072-3088
7. Criticism and interpretation: Shakespeare, PR 2965-3088
6. Shakesepare, William, PR 2750-3112
4. The drama: English literature, PR 2411-3195
2. English literature, PR
1. Philology and literature, P

This treatment of superordinate terms as sub-headings is basic to chain indexing. Kennedy incorporates this concept in his definition of chain indexing.

> There are no references from the greater to the lesser in a classified catalogue but the entries in the subject index are, in fact, all references, they refer to the appropriate number in the catalogue. And for a specific subject there must be a

pyramid of subject index entries. This method of providing references for the comprehensive subjects containing the specific subject, when applied to an index, is now known as chain indexing, a simple and expressive term.[23]

In this sense a chain index conforms to Cutter's concept of specific entry. Palmer and Wells state, "The systematic order of the classification relieves us, therefore, of the necessity to proceed from the general to the specific in any entry in the index."[24] Subject headings often demonstrate specificity by subdivisions as the Shakespeare example in the previous chapter demonstrates. Marie Prevost's noun theory of subject headings directly calls for specificity in the sub-headings.[25] This is not the case with chain indexing as Mills postulates,

> It is a fundamental rule of chain indexing that qualifying terms must be taken from terms *above* the indexing term in the chain, and never from terms below. The terms below represent *divisions* of the subject.[26]

This appears to be one of the most difficult concepts about chain indexing for students to understand. The investigator has discerned the problem when teaching students how to chain index. Students feel they should qualify main headings with subordinate headings not superordinate headings. In addition to the attachment of superordinate sub-headings this leads to possibilities of adjunction and expansion. Doughty demonstrates adjunction in the following contraction transformation.

> Index entries, as has been seen, usually form a chain of increasingly general, defining, terms like
> Graph: Electrical excitation: Brain: Physiology.
> But in this example the chain should obviously be replaced by a single substantive:
> Electro-encephalograph.
> The cataloguer should always be ready to replace chains by familiar or technical terms of this kind, but he should also remember to index the terms replaced—Electrical excitation, Excitation, Brain, Physiology, etc.
>
> How far compounds of nouns and adjectives should be broken up into chains of nouns is generally a matter for individual decision. Too much breaking up can become pedantic. On the other hand, the breaking up does facilitate the grouping of entries of the same specific topic where it appears under different general heads.[27]

Expansion may be discerned from the following statement by John Sharp.

> To aid chain indexing of adjectival phrases, in the schedules substantives are repeated after each qualifying adjective:
>
> | Nu | Moment |
> |----|--------|
> | Nub | Pitching moment |
> | Nud | Rolling moment |
> | Nuf | Yawing moment[28] |

Expansion may be seen as directly related to supplying grammatical context as well as being related to assumed context. Mills allows the indexer in steps 3 and 4 as well as 6 to consider the assumed context of the user.

In direct relationship to this step as well as step 3 is step 7 which allows synonyms to be present.

> 7. Synonyms are indexed directly to the class number, with a few exceptions.[29]

Mills points out the exceptions in the following statement.

> *Step 3* also demonstrates the rare occasion when a *see* reference is used. "England: Law" is clearly a synonym. But to make another entry under "England" for every entry beginning with "Great Britain" would involve serious duplication and the reference "England, *see* Great Britain" is used instead.
>
> Another example of this is when the last link in the chain is a common subdivision, e. g., Law, or Directories; these are given a general reference only, e.g., Directories of special subjects *see* name of subject. Apart from this, form divisions are not indexed, being considered unsought links.[30]

The inclusion of synonyms would allow the example of chain indexing to have rotational entries at entries 1 and 7.

11. Immediate constituents: Syntax: Shakespeare, PR 3078
10. Syntax: Shakespeare, PR 3078
9. Grammar: Shakespeare, PR 3075-3081
8. Language: Criticism: Shakespeare, PR 3072-3088
7. Criticism and interpretation: Shakespeare, PR 2965-3088
7. Interpretation and criticism: Shakespeare, PR 2965-3088
6. Shakespeare, William, PR 2750-3112
4. The drama: English literature, PR 2411-3195
2. English literature, PR
1. Philology and literature, P
1. Literature and philology, P

Classification terminology may be made current in the chain index as a result of this rule. Herrick notes this advantage in any index to a classified catalog.

> Among other benefits of the classified catalog in fields such as psychology, economics, anthropology, etc., where few concepts are being developed and where new terminology is rapidly appearing, the flexibility of the index terminology renders results of higher quality and is more responsive to the reader's need.[31]

By using this rule for synonyms to bring terminology up-to-date, the index may have entries under both current and former terms. This is a major advance other subject headings. Scheerer cautions against incorrect use of current terminology.

For that reason "bringing a subject heading up to date" has
become a deplorable practice. Changing the heading does
not bring up to date the books that belonged under the older
concept. Unless the change is made from a current term to a
more exact synonym, it entails in most cases a falsification
of subject material and bibliographical fact.[32]

Mills' eighth step is another general statement.

8. It should be realized, of course, that an index entry is made
for a subject only once.[33]

In summary of Mills' eight procedures or steps, the first two are preliminary
classificatory analysis steps; 5 and 8 are general statements; 3, 4, 6 and 7 are
basic rules for chain indexing. Obviously in practice, 3, 4, 6 and 7 may all be
applied simultaneously. Further it may be noted that precise morphological,
syntactical, lexical and contextual rules are not present. Also these procedures
do not provide for the obviously necessary summary cards and feature cards
of a classified catalog. It is, of course, here that many of the unsought links
are most useful.

Feature headings may be derived directly during the chain indexing
procedure. These are guide cards for the classified catalog. Ranganathan
points this out,

The Feature Headings can be got by Chain Procedure. They
are got by translating each successive digit in the class number
into its equivalent term in the natural language, proceeding
from left to right. This is just the reverse of what we do in
using Chain Procedure to arrive at the sequence of Headings and
Sub-headings in the Class Index Entry. A Feature Heading is
to consist of the part of the Class Number ending with the
digit contributing to the Feature Heading followed by the
equivalent term in the Favoured Language.

When consecutive Feature Headings stand together without
being separated by entries, the term corresponding to the
last digit in the Class Number may be sufficient.[34]

Or as Palmer and Wells state,

This indicates that, provided a translation is made at every
step, whether or not any entry exists there at a given moment,
the only digit of a class number which needs to be translated
is that on the extreme right. The translation of the notational
entry word in this manner is known as *featuring.*[35]

Another question which is left unanswered by Mills' principles although
not by his other writings is the depth or width of a chain index. Should a
term be entered only once? Should a term be allowed one but not two
synonyms? How are synonymous phrases treated? Is rotation of phrases
always a case of inversion? MacCallum Walker states,

Most of those who have written on the question of chain-
indexing have stressed that it is an economical method, i.e.

116

by following a fixed method it is possible to produce a subject-index that is quite adquate, without excessive use of synonyms, etc. as in other forms of subject-indexing. This economy, however, is merely an inner feature of the chain-indexing principle. There is a tendency to assume that the index produced on the lines of the examples in this paper is in itself adequate. It can not be too strongly emphasized that such is not the case if what is wanted is a means of helping readers to the utmost. The subject-entries produced by the chain-indexing procedure should be regarded as the *minimum* base upon which to build a satisfactory index to the classified catalogue.[36]

He further postulates,

The stages in the preparation of a sound and efficient subject-index are now three: (a) provision and selection of the basic entries on the chain-procedure method; (b) reversal of subject factors and inversion of most adjectival entries; (c) arrangement of entries as a relative index.[37]

Perreault discerns eight different types of indexes: "... *a*: alphabetico-directo subject headings, *b*: alphabetico-classed subject-headings, *c*: chain-index subject-headings, *d*: enumerative classification with relative index, *e*: faceted classification with index, *f*: permuted classed catalog with 'elementary' index, *g*: single-entry classed catalog with chain index, or even *h*: controlled unitermic post-coordinate indexing."[38] It appears that the combination of a chain index, a rotated index, and a relative index may be most valuable even if it must repeat the classified array at times.

ANALYSIS OF DATA COLLECTED

Certain basic problems faced the investigator in the collection of data for this section. Precisely what type of chain index was to be generated? Can a chain index be reversible if unsought links are discarded? Will the same rules govern the chain procedure for a classified catalog and an alphabetical subject catalog? In short what are the perimeters of the chain index and rules to be generated in this section?

In generating the chain index and rules in this section the investigator has accepted Mills' procedure as the basis for a chain index with inherent rotational relative factors. This may be called as MacCallum Walker does a minimum index.[39] If all terms are rotated, the index would certainly be longer. It would collect more distributed relatives in an analytical fashion. The resulting inversions would show not the most specific entry terms but rather the more generic terms coupled with the specific. This would be the equivalent of the summary cards in the classified catalog. Whether this would be useful in the index is open to question. Mills states,

Therefore, remembering that the function of the index is to display those relations not shown in the systematic order, the index should give entries such as *Drama: English literature* which will file alongside *Drama: German literature,* etc., thus collecting the distributed relatives. But it is *not* necessary to index *English drama, German drama,* etc.; for the analysis of English literature into English drama, English poetry, English fiction, etc., *has already been done in the classified file.*[40]

It should be noted that the expansion of the chain index to a full relative index may be similarly unnecessary. If a full relative index displays all the divisions of an entry, the index simply repeats the classification tables in a less orderly array. However if a relative index displays only those divisions of an entry not covered by the inclusive range of the entry's notation, the relative index is acting exactly like a chain index. Thus it seems to the investigator that the minimum index will be satisfactory for this section and its hypothesis.

The second basic problem deals with the purpose of this chain index. Is it to generate an index to a classified catalog or for a list of subject headings? Can this index be completely reversible and thus justify the third hypothesis? The first of these two questions can be easily answered. Chain index entries can be converted to subject headings. Ranganathan writes,

> The question then is: "Can there be an alternative set of Rules of Chain Procedure so as to retain such Classified Pockets in the Dictionary Catalogue?" I now find that the answer is "Yes." In fact, the Rules of Chain Procedure can be so framed as to yield several alternative patterns of arrangement of Subject Headings. Indeed the versatility of the Chain Procedure is greater than what has been realised during the early years of its use. If any pattern of arrangement whatever is clearly defined, a corresponding set of Rules of Chain Procedure can be framed. All that the Chain Procedure does is to mechanise the process of deriving the kind of Subject Headings implied by the pattern and to secure consistency in the pattern.[41]

Further explanation may be found in an article by Coates entitled "Use of *B.N.B.* in Dictionary Cataloguing."[42] The discarding of unsought links creates the major problem of reversibility of the index. In general Mills' procedure discards period divisions and general form divisions as unsought links. If these entries do not appear in the alphabetical array, then they would not appear in the classified version of the alphabetical array. Hence in this sense the Mills' chain index is not completely reversible. General form divisions present no problem other than quantity and can be included in a reversible chain index. By definition period divisions should also be included in a completely reversible chain index. There are far more problems in the case of period divisions than the case of general form divisions. General form divisions are simply terms—usually very generic terms—that are indexable. Period divisions may be terms, single years or ranges of years, e.g. modern, 1950, or

1900-60. Period divisions that are terms may not always be transformed into dates. What range of years is referred to by "modern"? When does the "medieval" period end? Even if this lexical problem can be resolved, a second problem remains. How useful would period entries be in an index? Their existence is dependent on their use in the classification system. An inquiry for all the material on a particular period or year could not necessarily rely solely on the period entries. The investigator's decision has been in general to exclude period divisions from the index. This decision is made as period divisions are sub-headings and are not indexable. They must, of course, appear as feature cards and could exist in a separate chronologically arranged index. General form divisions will be indexed except certain specified cases.

The following examples and rules result from chain indexing the range of numbers assigned to Shakespeare, PR 2750-3112. This range of numbers was chosen for the experimental model as a result of the previous analysis of Shakespeare's subject heading subdivisions in chapter four. This choice will allow comparisons between the subject heading subdivisions and the chain index main headings or ascriptors to be made. Each class number and Cutter number in this range of numbers was indexed by Mills' procedure with specific rules generated when necessary. Daily's rules were followed for structural form when applicable—especially rules 3, 5, 6, 7 and 8.[43]

PR 2750-3112 generated 564 index entries. 417 of these are main entries and are typed as capital letters; 145 are access entries or synonyms of main entries and are typed in normal upper and lower case fashion. In addition 26 rules have been generated. Only those entries which generated specific rules are included in the following examples. All rules are typed in capital letters.

The first number of Shakespeare's range of numbers is PR 2750. There are three divisions of this number represented by Cutter numbers. PR 2750 and its three divisions appear in the following example.

PR
2750   Original quartos and facsimiles and reprints.
        .A1-A73, Original editions.
            (Arranged and numbered like 2801-2873.)
        .B1-B73, Facsimiles and reprints.
            (Arranged like .A1-A73.)
        .C1-C9, Collected reprints.
            (Arranged chronologically.)

The classificatory display following Mills' first step for PR 2750 is:

STEP 1

1.	P	Philology and literature
2.	PR	English literature
3.	PR 2199-3195	English renaissance (1500-1640)
4.	PR 2411-3195	The drama
5.	PR 2417-3195	Individual authors
6.	PR 2750-3112	Shakespeare, William

7.	PR 2750	Original quartos and facsimiles and reprints.
8.	PR 2750.A1-A73	Original editions

As there are three coordinate divisions of entry 7, PR 2750, all three must be considered in analysing the number. The parenthetical notes following PR 2750.A1-A73 require the expansion of this number into 73 divisions. **Any parenthetical arrange-like notes in L. C. classification must be fully expanded in the preliminary classificatory display steps.** The expanded first step may now be represented in the following fashion: PR 2750.A1-A73 is arranged like PR 2801-2873 (the numbers assigned to the individual works of Shakespeare).

STEP 1

1.	P	Philology and literature.
2.	PR	English literature.
3.	PR 2199-3195	English renaissance (1500-1640).
4.	PR 2411-3195	The drama.
5.	PR 2417-3195	Individual authors.
6.	PR 2750-3112	Shakespeare, William.
7.	PR 2750	Original quartos and facsimiles and reprints.
8.	PR 2750.A1-A73	Original editions.
9.	PR 2750.A1	All's well that ends well.

As Mills' second step does not apply in this case, his third step may now be applied. Initially this step reverses the order of step 1. Each link must now be analysed for possible adjustment. Link 9 "All's well that ends well" is an acceptable title entry. **All titles listed in the classification schedule must be indexed directly.** This follows a general principle of Ranganathan[44] and is essential for a reversible index. Link 8 "Original editions" is acceptable because the specific element of the entry occurs in the initial index position. **An index entry consisting of an adjective and a noun is acceptable if the specific element, i.e. the distinguishing element, occurs in the initial index position.** This means that the specific element (an adjective) is derived from the underlying "Editions are original." The embedded element distinguishes the generic element; it is a division of the generic element. Link 7 "Original quartos and facsimiles and reprints" contains specific terms occurring further in the specificity, e.g. "Original," "facsimiles" and "reprints." These terms should be reserved for their specific entries. **If specific terms are embedded in more generic terms, reserve the specific terms for their own specific entries deleting them from the more generic terms.** Link 7 "Original quartos and facsimiles and reprints" may be transformed to "Quartos." Link 6 "Shakespeare, William" presents the basic problem of proper personal names. Daily's rule 13 calls for personal names to "follow the rules of entry of authors' names."[45] However, "Shakespeare, William" may be transformed by contraction to "Shakespeare." **If the proper personal name of any author is distinctly known by only the surname, the surname may be used as the index term.** The form of link 5 is acceptable just as link 8's form was. Link 4 "The drama" does not follow Daily's rule 4.

To distinguish between "Church" as an organized body and various kinds of churches, use the definite article, for example, *The Church,* for the former definition and *Churches* for the latter. Employ the definite article with the noun form of adjectives (substantives).[46]

Link 4 may be transformed simply to "Drama." Link 3 "English renaissance (1500-1640)" presents the previously mentioned problem of period division. However its form is basically acceptable. There is no need to adjust the form of the parenthetical dates if this link will probably be discarded. "English literature" link 2 is acceptable just as links 8 and 5 were. Link 1 "Philology and literature" is an instance of co-ordination (_____ and _____). **The co-ordination of two terms such as (_____ and _____) is indexed with the first term as index entry and the second term as access entry if this may be done without removing contextual meaning from either term.**

STEP 3

9.	PR 2750.A1	ALL'S WELL THAT ENDS WELL.
8.	PR 2750.A1-A73	ORIGINAL EDITIONS.
7.	PR 2750	QUARTOS.
6.	PR 2750-3112	SHAKESPEARE.
5.	PR 2417-3195	INDIVIDUAL AUTHORS.
4.	PR 2411-3195	DRAMA.
3.	PR 2199-3195	ENGLISH RENAISSANCE (1500-1640).
2.	PR	ENGLISH LITERATURE.
1.	P	PHILOLOGY.
1.	P	Literature.

Mills' fourth step calls for determination of false links and unsought links. This is basically an exclusion rule. As the exclusion of unsought links may be highly subjective matter, the following objective principle is stated. **All period divisions except the terms ancient and medieval and their equivalents will be considered subordinate subdivisions and not retained. All general form divisions will be retained unless they are specifically listed on an "exclude list."** These rules cause link 3 "English renaissance (1500-1640)" to be excluded. Secondly link 5 "Individual authors" will be added to the "exclude list" as it is merely an internal division in the structure of the classification system.

STEP 4

9.	PR 2750.A1	ALL'S WELL THAT ENDS WELL.
8.	PR 2750.A1-A73	ORIGINAL EDITIONS.
7.	PR 2750	QUARTOS.
6.	PR 2750-3112	SHAKESPEARE.
5.		
4.	PR 2411-3195	DRAMA.
3.		
2.	PR	ENGLISH LITERATURE.
1.	P	PHILOLOGY.
1.	P	Literature.

Mills' step 5 does apply to this analysis as all steps that are indexable are being indexed.

The contextual principle, Mills' step 6, has already been generated in the second chapter. **If the contextual meaning of a term is dependent on the location of that term in the classified array, the most specific hierarchical term that will supply that context must be added as a contextual link following the index term.** Not all terms resulting in chain indexing must be retained in the final alphabetical index. Only those terms necessary to retain the contextual meaning of the specific index term must be retained. This rule implies that index terms should not have subordinate sub-headings but rather should have superordinate sub-headings. **Avoid a classified array in the alphabetical array. Sub-headings must be superordinate and not subordinate or co-ordinate.** The total context of link 9 is "All's Well That Ends Well": Original Editions: Quartos: Shakespeare: Drama: English Literature: Philology." In following the contextual rule "Original Editions" must be present to distinguish between original editions of *All's Well* from facsimiles and reprints: "Quartos" must be present to separate quartos and folios; "Shakespeare" must be present to distinguish authorship. The other steps may be considered as assumed context of the English reader. The total contextual links are obviously more objective than this reduction. This step implies a judgmental factor. The total links would probably be acceptable in a mechanical system. The reduction would be more acceptable in a manual, visual system.

STEP 6

9. ALL'S WELL THAT ENDS WELL: ORIGINAL EDITIONS:
    QUARTOS: SHAKESPEARE, PR 2750.A1
8. ORIGINAL EDITIONS: QUARTOS: SHAKESPEARE, PR 2750.A1-A73.
7. QUARTOS: SHAKESPEARE, PR 2750.
6. SHAKESPEARE, PR 2750-3112
4. DRAMA: ENGLISH LITERATURE, PR 2411-3195.
2. ENGLISH LITERATURE, PR.
1. PHILOLOGY, P.
1. Literature, P.

Link 4 "Drama: English Literature, PR 2411-3195" may cause the reader some consternation. Obviously this is only English drama of 1500 to 1640. The temptation is to resurrect the unsought period divisions. This would be unacceptable to the rules of step 4 as well as repeating the classified array in the alphabetical array. Link 4 stands as a logically true statement. It is not an exclusive statement but rather one of a class of true statements about English drama.

Step 7 allows the inclusion of synonyms. **Synonyms are one form of access term.** The only necessary synonym appears to be "British literature" for "English literature."

PR 2750.A1 proved to be a most fruitful entry. It generated eleven separate rules. The remaining entries all begin their generation at link 7 as links 6-1 will be repeated for each of them. The following rules were generated by the remaining entries. PR 2750.A40 is derived from PR 2840 which reads "Lost play: Love's labour's won."

STEP 1

7.   PR 2750   QUARTOS.
8.   PR 2750.A1-A73 ORIGINAL EDITIONS.
9.   PR 2750.A40   Lost play: Love's labour's won.

The title to be indexed is obviously "Love's Labour's Won." The phrase "lost play" is a dependent synonym for the title. It is simply descriptive of what the title is.

STEP 3

9.   PR 2750.A40   LOVE'S LABOUR'S WON.
8.   PR 2750.A1-A73 ORIGINAL EDITIONS.
7.   PR 2750   QUARTOS.

If a descriptive synonym cannot be separated from an independent term or phrase, then the synonym is dependent and should not be indexed: if the independent term or phrase loses its contextual meaning because of this separation, the term or phrase is not independent and should not be separated.

STEP 6

9.   LOVE'S LABOUR'S WON: ORIGINAL EDITIONS: QUARTOS: SHAKESPEARE, PR 2750.A40.
8.   ORIGINAL EDITIONS: QUARTOS: SHAKESPEARE, PR 2750.A1-A73.
7.   QUARTOS: SHAKESPEARE, PR 2750.

PR 2750.A42 is derived from PR 2842 which is part of the range of numbers PR 2841-2849 for Shakespeare's poems. PR 2842 reads "Selections. Anthologies."

STEP 1

7.   PR 2750   QUARTOS.
8.   PR 2750.A1-A73 ORIGINAL EDITIONS.
9.   PR 2750.A41-49 Poems.
10.   PR 2750.A42   Selections. Anthologies.

In a co-ordinate series of classification terms the first acceptable term is chosen as the index entry and any others are retained as access terms.

STEP 3

10.   PR 2750.A42   SELECTIONS.
9.   PR 2750.A41-49 POEMS
8.   PR 2750.A1-A73 ORIGINAL EDITIONS.
7.   PR 2750   QUARTOS.

Due to the different meanings applied to "selection" and "selected works" by the Library of Congress it is necessary to retain the distinctness of each term. **"Selected Works" refers to a limited number of complete works contained in a single collection. "Selections" refers to a limited number of complete or partial works contained in a single collection.**

10.   SELECTIONS: POEMS: ORIGINAL EDITIONS: QUARTOS:
      SHAKESPEARE, PR 2750.A42.
10.   Anthologies: POEMS: ORIGINAL EDITIONS: QUARTOS:
      SHAKESPEARE, PR 2750.A42
9.   POEMS: ORIGINAL EDITIONS: QUARTOS: SHAKESPEARE,
      PR 2750.A41-A49.

The following classification is "PR 2843 Special poems."

STEP 1

7.	PR 2750	QUARTOS.
8.	PR 2750.A1-A73	ORIGINAL EDITIONS.
9.	PR 2750.A41-A49	POEMS.
10.	PR 2750.A43	Special poems.

"Special" is used as an internal classification scheme descriptor and should be added to the "exclude list."

STEP 4

10.		
9.	PR 2750.A41-A49	POEMS.
8.	PR 2750.A1-A73	ORIGINAL EDITIONS.
7.	PR 2750	QUARTOS.

All unsought links should be used as feature terms in the classified array. Feature terms do not need contextual links as sub-headings. Link 10 appears as "Special poems, PR 2750.A43" in the classified array only.
The last classification heading in this sequence is "PR 2849 Other."

STEP 1

7.	PR 2750	QUARTOS.
8.	PR 2750.A1-A73	ORIGINAL EDITIONS.
9.	PR 2750.A41-A49	POEMS.
10.	PR 2750.A49	Other.

As the word "Other" is an unacceptable index term, the following manipulation is necessary. First the hierarchy for the "Other" is clearly established: second an individual member of the "Other" class is isolated if possible and chosen for the index term. "Lover's Complaint" is a possible individual member of this class of other poems.

STEP 4

10.	PR 2750.A49L6	LOVER'S COMPLAINT.
9.	PR 2750.A41-A49	POEMS.
8.	PR 2750.A1-A73	ORIGINAL EDITIONS.
7.	PR 2750	QUARTOS.

"Other" is thus added to the exclude list and a feature entry made for it.
The next section of the classification is PR 2851-2875 "Doubtful, spurious works. 'Shakespeare apocrypha.' "

7.   PR 2750   QUARTOS.
8.   PR 2750.A1-A73   ORIGINAL EDITIONS.
9.   PR 2750.A51-A73   Doubtful, spurious works.
                        "Shakespeare apocrypha."

If two or more adjectives qualify a single noun in a co-ordinate or synonymous sense, so that two or more noun phrases are embedded in one noun phrase, the two or more noun phrases should be separated and the phrase most commonly used in the literature of the subject is chosen as the index entry with the others as access terms. This means that "Spurious works" is chosen as the index entry and "Doubtful works" as an access entry. "Shakespeare apocrypha" is another access entry.

STEP 6

9.   SPURIOUS WORKS: ORIGINAL EDITIONS: QUARTOS:
      SHAKESPEARE, PR 2750.A51-A73.

9.   Doubtful works: ORIGINAL EDITIONS: QUARTOS:
      SHAKESPEARE, PR 2750.A51-A73.

9.   Shakespeare apocrypha: ORIGINAL EDITIONS: QUARTOS,
      PR 2750.A51-A73.

PR 2751 is the first number in the range of numbers for collected works, PR 2751-2754. Although PR 2751 has no individual classification heading, an analysis of the hierarchy demonstrates that this number is being used in a parallel fashion to PR 2750. PR 2751 is for folios just as PR 2750 is for quartos.

	Collected works.
2751.A1	First folio edition (1623).
.A15	Facsimiles, by date of reprint.
.A2	Second folio edition (1632).
.A25	Facsimiles.
.A3	Third folio edition (1664).
.A35	Facsimiles
.A4	Fourth folio edition (1685).
.A45	Facsimiles.
(.A6-Z)	Collations, notes, descriptions, etc., of the folio editions, see Z8811-8813.

PR 2751 "Folios" is a missing link. **In the preliminary classification display steps, any missing links should be displayed. Parallel sections of the classification should be displayed in a parallel fashion.**

STEP 2
7.   PR 2751   FOLIOS.
8.   PR 2751   FACSIMILES.

PR 2751 (.A6-Z) is a shelf list number in L. C. classification.

| 7. | PR 2751 | FOLIOS. |
| 8. | PR 2751 (.A6-Z) | Collations, notes, descriptions, etc., of the folio editions, see Z8811-8813. |

Shelf list numbers in the classification should be naturally indexed as synonyms with a "use" note to the correct number.

STEP 7

8. Collations: FOLIOS: SHAKESPEARE, PR 2751 (.A6-Z) *USE* Z8811-8813.
8. Descriptive bibliography: FOLIOS: SHAKESPEARE, PR 2751 (.A6-Z) *USE* Z8811-8813.

Any useful term or phrase with the same lexical meaning may be used as a synonym.

PR 2752-54 are the range of numbers for editions of the collected works with commentary. The classification heading is "Editions, with commentary, etc."

STEP 1

| 7. | PR 2751-54 | COLLECTED WORKS. |
| 8. | PR 2752-54 | Editions, with commentary, etc. |

The specific element of this heading is "commentary" not "editions."
The most specific term should always be the entry element.

STEP 3

| 8. | PR 2752-54 | COMMENTARIES. |
| 7. | PR 2751-54 | COLLECTED WORKS. |

The "with" in the above example may be deleted without loss of contextual meaning. **If syntactical terms or phrases may be deleted without loss of contextual meaning, this should be done.**

STEP 6

8. COMMENTARIES: COLLECTED WORKS: SHAKESPEARE, PR 2752-54.
7. COLLECTED WORKS: SHAKESPEARE, PR 2751-54.

PR 2775 is the number for Dutch translations of Shakespeare. It is stated simply as "Dutch" in the classified tables.

STEP 1

| 7. | PR 2775-2800 | Translations. |
| 8. | PR 2775-2776 | Dutch. |

If the main heading is simply an adjective which may be naturally combined with the next higher link, this should be done.

STEP 6

8. DUTCH TRANSLATIONS: SHAKESPEARE, PR 2775-2776.
7. TRANSLATIONS: SHAKESPEARE, PR 2775-2800.

PR 2796 is the number for Asian translations of Shakespeare. The classification heading reads "Asia."

STEP 1

7.	PR 2775-2800	TRANSLATIONS.
8.	PR 2796-2800	Other language.
9.	PR 2796	Asia.

Whenever an obvious adjectival form of an adjectival noun is available in the natural language and its use would allow two links to be combined, it should be used.

STEP 6

9. ASIAN TRANSLATIONS: SHAKESPEARE, PR 2796
8.
7. TRANSLATIONS: SHAKESPEARE, PR 2775-2800.

The individual works of Shakespeare, PR 2801-2840, are subdivided by the following internal table.

	Texts.
.A1	By date.
.A2A-Z.	By editor (or actor).
.A25,	Adaptations for school performance.
.A3A-Z,	Selections. By editor.
	Translations.
(.A4A-Z)	French, see PR 2779.
(.A5A-Z)	German, see PR 2782.
(.A6A-Z)	Other. By language, see PR 2776-2795.
.A8-Z,	Criticism.

All internal and external auxiliary tables should only be expanded as they represent the holdings of an individual collection. Useful general references resulting from internal or external auxiliary tables may be added to the index. The following general references may be made:

Selections: Individual works *SEE* Title of individual work.
Criticism: Individual works *SEE* Title of individual work.

PR 2877-2879 is the range of numbers for "Imitations, paraphrases, adaptations."

STEP 1

7. PR 2877-2879   Imitations, paraphrases, adaptations.

As it has proven desirable to reduce such a series of terms to index terms and access terms, the following rule is generated. **If in a co-ordinate series of classification terms, the first listed term has undesirable ambiguity when stated alone or is not the term commonly used in the literature, another of the terms in the series may be selected as the index term. All the other terms will, of course, be retained for consideration as access terms.**

7.   PR 2877-2879   PARAPHRASES.
7.   PR 2877-2879   Imitations.
7.   PR 2877-2879   Adaptations.

INTERPRETATIONS AND CONCLUSIONS

The range of numbers for Shakespeare, PR 2750-3112, generated a
total of 564 entries for a chain index. There are 417 main index entries,
145 access entries, and 2 general references. In addition 93 feature headings
for the classified array were generated. 26 rules for chain indexing were
written. These rules will be discussed and analysed in detail in the next
chapter. The chain index was tested for indexability and morphology.

The following tables demonstrate the analysis of the chain index for
indexability. As all the index headings were generated from the classification
headings, no separate table is given for this comparison; however, class
numbers, Cutter numbers and feature headings are shown.

CLASS NUMBERS

	Total	Individual Numbers	Ranges
Classification headings	262	256	6
Index headings	236	185	51

CUTTER NUMBERS

	Total	Individual Numbers	Ranges
Classification headings	180	178	2
Index headings	190	182	8

FEATURE HEADINGS

	Total	Individual Numbers	Ranges
Class numbers without periods	55	42	13
Period class numbers	28	24	4
Cutter numbers	10	6	4

These tables show that 90% of the class numbers are indexed by individual
number entries or ranges of numbers. All the Cutter numbers are indexed.
The feature headings show the individual unindexed sections which are all
covered by some type of indexing. The period divisions represent 9% of the
class numbers. This means that the class numbers indexed plus the period
divisions on feature cards equals 99% possibility for a reversible index.

Obviously the chain index demonstrates superior indexability to the existing indexes to L. C. classification.

The form of the entire ascriptor was analysed for the number of sub-headings. This was done for both index entries and access entries.

NUMBER OF SUB-HEADINGS

	None	One	Two	Three	Four	Five
Index entries	3	127	133	108	46	0
Access entries	7	43	55	32	8	0

This shows that the number of sub-headings is consistently one, two or three. The number of sub-headings is thus predictable.

The final test applied to the index was for the morphology of the main index headings and access headings. The sub-headings were not included as all the sub-headings are also main headings.

MORPHOLOGY TEST

	Titles	W	W_aW	W_aW_aW	Proper	Other
Main headings	196	121	67	14	18	6
Access headings	42	66	22	1	2	11

As the titles were accepted directly and as they represent separate problems, they were counted separately and not included in the following interpretations. This analysis shows that 85% of the main headings and 85% of the access headings are in the form of W or W_aW. It may be further observed that the four forms, W, W_aW, W_aW_aW and Proper nouns, represent 99% of the main headings. The rules for chain indexing thus allow a 99% predictability for the morphology of the main headings.

These tests have shown predictability of chain indexing in regard to morphology, form, and indexability. The use of the feature cards allows the chain index to be a reversible index. The ascriptors represent contextually extracted classification headings which could serve equally well as subject headings or alphabetical index headings.

[1] S. R. Ranganathan, *Theory of Library Catalogue* (Madras: Madras Library Association, 1938), pp. 114-118: 164-165.

[2] S. R. Ranganathan, *Classified Catalogue Code with Additional Rules for Dictionary Catalogue Code,* Assisted by A. Neelameghan (New York: Asia Publishing House, 1964), p. 46.

[3] Mills, "Chain Indexing and the Classified Catalogue," *op. cit.,* p. 141-148.

[4] International Federation for Documentation. *Proceedings of the International Study Conference on Classification for Information Retrieval, op. cit.,* pp. 103-104; Mills, *A Modern Outline of Library Classification, loc. cit.*; Mills, "Indexing a Classification Shceme," *op. cit.,* pp. 40-48; British Standards Institution. *Guide to the Universal Decimal Classification* (UDC), B. S. 1000C: 1963, F. I. D. No. 345; (London: British Standards Institution, 1963), pp. 33-41.

[5] Kennedy, *op. cit.,* pp. 71-72.

[6] Bernard I. Palmer and A. S. Wells, *The Fundamentals of Library Classification* (London: George Allen and Unwin Ltd., 1951), pp. 104-105.

[7] C. D. Batty, "Chain Indexing," *Encyclopedia of Library and Information Science,* (New York: Marcel Dekker, Inc., 1970?) IV, ?.

[8] Mills, Chain Indexing," *op. cit.,* p. 143.

[9] *Idem.*

[10] *Supra,* p. 36, fn. 86.

[11] Mills, "Chain Indexing," *loc. cit.*

[12] *Ibid.,* p. 142.

[13] Scheerer, *loc. cit.*

[14] Mills, "Chain Indexing," *op. cit.,* p. 145.

[15] *Ibid.,* p. 143.

[16] Mills, "Indexing a Classification Scheme," *op. cit.,* p. 145.

[17] E. J. Coates, "The Use of B.N.B. in Dictionary Cataloguing," *Library Association Record,* LIX (June, 1957), 199.

[18] Langridge, *op. cit.,* p. 191.

[19] Herrick, "Development of a Classified Catalog," *op. cit.,* p. 424.

[20] Mills, "Chain Indexing," *op. cit.,* p. 143.

[21] *Idem.*

[22] *Ibid.,* p. 144.

[23] Kennedy, *op. cit.,* p. 33.

[24] Palmer and Wells, *op. cit.,* p. 102.

[25] Prevost, "An Approach to Theory," *op. cit.,* p. 149.

[26] Mills, "Indexing a Classification Scheme," *op. cit.,* p. 43.

[27] Doughty, *op. cit.*, pp. 176-177.

[28] Vickery, *op. cit.*, p. 98.

[29] Mills, "Chain Indexing," *op. cit.*, p. 143.

[30] *Ibid.*, p. 144.

[31] Herrick, "Classified Catalog," *op. cit.*, p. 292.

[32] Scheerer, *op. cit.*, p. 198.

[33] Mills, "Chain Indexing," *op. cit.*, p. 143.

[34] Ranganathan, *Classified Catalogue Code, op. cit.*, p. 324.

[35] Palmer and Wells, *op. cit.*, p. 106.

[36] MacCallum Walker, *op. cit.*, p. 265.

[37] *Ibid.*, pp. 266-267.

[38] Perreault, *Reclassification, Rationale and Problems, op. cit.*, p. 189.

[39] MacCallum Walker, *loc. cit.*

[40] Mills, "Chain Indexing," *op. cit.*, pp. 141-142.

[41] Ranganathan, *Classified Catalogue Code, op. cit.*, p. 330.

[42] Coates, "The Use of B.N.B. in Dictionary Cataloguing," *op. cit.*, p. 330.

[43] Daily, "The Grammar of Subject Headings," *loc. cit.*

[44] Ranganathan, *Dictionary Catalogue Code* (Madras Library Association Publication Series, 14; Madras: Thompson, 1945), p. 182.

[45] Daily, "The Grammar of Subject Headings," *op. cit.*, p. 156.

[46] *Ibid.*, p. 153.

CHAPTER VI

DEVELOPMENT OF THE ARGUMENT FOR APPLICATION OF THE RULES TO ADDITIONAL EXAMPLES

ANALYSIS OF THE DATA COLLECTED

The twenty-six rules and the exclude list developed in the previous chapter were applied to six limited sections of the classification. Each section was chosen to exhibit different problem areas. No new rules were generated and the exclude list was expanded by only eight terms. The six examples represented 157 class numbers and 11 Cutter numbers which generated 147 index entries and 57 access entries.

QA 1-115, mathematics, was chosen as the first example to test the rules generated from Shakespeare on a subject in the pure sciences. The second example, PR 5360-5368, the range of numbers for George Bernard Shaw, was chosen to test the rules on an author with far fewer numbers than Shakespeare. The first 99 numbers for Epigraphy CN 1-99, were chosen as they display a very full range of general form divisions. SF 600-775, part of the range of numbers for veterinary medicine, was chosen as an example of the applied sciences. UH 20-399 was selected because it represents a semantically wide range of numbers for miscellaneous military services. The sixth example was chosen from the classificatory references of the sa headings under the subject heading Heraldry. The following tables demonstrate the data collected and its analysis.

ADDITIONAL EXAMPLES

Example From	Index Terms	Access Terms	Feature Headings	Class Numbers	Cutter Numbers
QA	46	20	18	46	3
PR	9	1	3	6	5
CN	19	11	6	20	2
SF	27	6	16	34	0
UH	29	5	23	30	1
Heraldry	17	14	0	15	0
TOTAL	147	57	66	157	11

SUMMARY TABLE

	Class Numbers	Cutter Numbers
Classification headings	157	11
Index headings	137	10

These tables show that 87% of the class numbers are indexed directly. 99% of the Cutter numbers are indexed. The feature headings show the individual unindexed sections which are all covered by some type of indirect indexing. The period divisions represent 11% of the class numbers. This means that the class numbers indexed plus the period divisions on feature cards equals 98% possibility for a reversible index. Again the chain index demonstrates a greater unity of vocabulary than the existing indexes to L. C. classification.

As was done in the previous chapter, the form of the entire ascriptor was analysed for the number of sub-headings.

NUMBER OF SUB-HEADINGS

	None	One	Two	Three	Four	Five
Index entries	11	105	26	5	0	0
Access entries	1	42	14	0	0	0

This shows that the number of sub-headings is consistently one or two. In fact in this sample 71% of the index headings have only one subheading. The number of sub-headings is again predictable.

The third test applied to group of headings just as to the Shakespeare index was for the morphology of the main index headings and access headings.

MORPHOLOGY TEST

	Titles	W	W_aW	W_aW_aW	Proper	Other
Main headings	4	77	41	5	15	5
Access headings	0	43	11	0	0	3

As the titles were previously exluded in the Shakespeare analysis, they are not included in the following interpretations. This analysis shows that 83% of the main headings and 95% of the access headings are in the form of W or W_aW. It may be further observed that the four forms, W, W_aW, W_aW_aW and Proper nouns, represent 94% of the main headings and 95% of the access headings. The rules for chain indexing in this example allow a 94% predictability for the morphology of the main headings.

In further analysing the data collected in this chapter and the previous one, it appears that the twenty-six rules are adequate for chain indexing L. C. classification. Those rules may now be restated.

Three rules were generated for Mills first two steps. These are the rules dealing with the preliminary classificatory display. They may be called the *hierarchical display steps.*

2:1   In the preliminary classificatory display steps, any missing links should be displayed. Parallel sections of the classification should be displayed in a parallel fashion.

2:2   Any parenthetical arrange-like notes in L. C. classification must be fully expanded in the preliminary classificatory display steps.

2:3   All internal and external auxiliary tables should only be expanded as they represent the holdings of an individual collection. Useful general references resulting from internal or external auxiliary tables may be added to the index.

Rule 2:3 is necessary if the character of L. C. classification is to be retained. The index could hardly develop all the potential numbers.

Mills' step 3 is concerned with the adjustment of the vocabulary. Thirteen rules were developed for this step. This is basically a *morphologic step* dealing with the acceptability of form.

3:1   The most specific term should always be the entry element.

3:2   The co-ordination of two terms such as (_____ and _____) is indexed with the first term as index entry and the second term as access entry if this may be done without removing contextual meaning from either term.

3:3   In a co-ordinate series of classification terms the first acceptable term is chosen as the index entry and any others are retained as access terms.

3:4   If in a co-ordinate series of classification terms, the first listed term has undesirable ambiguity when stated alone or is not the term commonly used in the literature, another of the terms in the series may be selected as the index term. All the other terms will, of course, be retained for consideration as access terms.

3:5   If specific terms are embedded in more generic terms, reserve the specific terms for their own specific entries deleting them from the more generic terms.

3:6   If a descriptive synonym cannot be separated from an independent term or phrase, then the synonym is dependent and should not be indexed; if the independent term or phrase loses its contextual meaning because of this separation, the term or phrase is not independent and should not be separated.

3:7   An index entry consisting of an adjective and a noun is acceptable if the specific element, i.e. the distinguishing element, occurs in the initial index position.

3:8   If two or more adjectives qualify a single noun in a co-ordinate or synonymous sense, so that two or more noun phrases are embedded in one noun phrase, the two or more noun phrases should be separated and the phrase most commonly used in the literature of the subject is chosen as the index entry with the others as access terms.

3:9   If the main heading is simply an adjective which may be naturally combined with the next higher link, this should be done.

3:10   If syntactical terms or phrases may be deleted without loss of contextual meaning, this should be done.

3:11   "Selected works" refers to a limited number of complete works contained in a single collection. "Selections" refers to a limited number of complete or partial works contained in a single collection.

3:12   If the proper personal name of any author is distinctly known by only the surname, the surname may be used as the index term.

3:13   All titles listed in the classification schedule must be indexed directly.

These thirteen rules are most important as they control the morphologic basis of the chain index before adding the contextual sub-headings of step 6. The application of these rules accounts for the high degree of predictable morphology shown in all the examples analysed.

Step 4 is the basic weeding step of chain indexing. This step deals with the removal of unsought terms and false links. It may be considered both a *lexical step* and a *graphemic step.*

4:1   All period divisions except the terms ancient and medieval and their equivalents will be considered subordinate subdivisions and not retained.

4:2   All general form divisions will be retained unless they are specifically listed on an "exclude list."

4:3   As the word "other" is an unacceptable index term, the following manipulation is necessary. First the hierarchy for the "other" is clearly established; second an individual member of the "other" class is isolated if possible and chosen for the index term.

4:4   All unsought links should be used as feature terms in the classified array. Feature terms do not need contextual links as sub-headings.

The following exclude list has been generated by the 610 class and Cutter numbers already indexed. The use of this list makes this step a *graphemic step.*

EXCLUDE LIST

By country	Minor
By editor	Miscellaneous
By form	Nonofficial
Cf.	Official
Collective	Other
Essays	Other countries
General	Separate works
General minor	Serial
General special	Special
History (as a form, not a subject)	Subarranged
Including +	Texts
Individual	

The use of a specific exclude list is basic if there is to be consistent indexing of general form divisions. Individual terms must be isolated rather than trying to follow general principles.

Mills' step 6 is considered as the attachment of any necessary superordinate terms to provide contextual linkage. This step may be considered the *semantic* or *contextual step.*

135

6:1   If the contextual meaning of a term is dependent on the location of that term in the classified array, the most specific hierarchical term that will supply that context must be added as a contextual link following the index term.

6:2   Avoid a classified array in the alphabetical array. Sub-headings must be superordinate and not subordinate or co-ordinate.

6:3   Whenever an obvious adjectival form of an adjectival noun is available in the natural language and its use would allow two links to be combined, it should be used.

The seventh step allows synonyms to be present in the chain index. These rules are designed to expand this step to include all access terms—both synonyms and access terms generated by the rules in step 3. This step may be considered as another *lexical step.*

7:1   Synonyms are one form of access term.

7:2   Any useful term or phrase with the same lexical meaning may be used as a synonym.

7:3   Shelf list numbers in the classification should be naturally indexed as synonyms with a "USE" note to the correct number.

It should be noted that these twenty-six rules were all generated by the first half of the range of numbers for Shakespeare. The second half of Shakespeare's range and the six additional examples have all tested these rules. Although some portions of the classification may require additional rules, the investigator believes these rules represent the basic rules for chain indexing L. C. classification.

INTERPRETATIONS AND CONCLUSIONS

Although the results of the individual additional example have already been interpreted in the first part of this chapter, the sixth example is particularly worthy of further consideration. This example based on the *sa* headings for the subject heading *Heraldry* shows dramatically the values of chain indexing. The following table compares the subject headings and the chain index headings for this example.

COMPARISON TABLE OF SUBJECT HEADINGS
AND CHAIN INDEX HEADINGS FOR HERALDRY

Subject Headings	Chain Index Headings
Heraldry	HERALDRY, CR.
Achievements (Heraldry)	(∅)
Badges	DEVICES: HERALDRY, CR 67-69.
	Badges: HERALDRY, CR 67-69.
Battle-cries	BATTLE CRIES: HERALDRY, CR 79.
Chivalry	CHIVALRY: HERALDRY, CR 4501-6305.

Subject Headings	Chain Index Headings
Color in heraldry	(∅)
Crests	CRESTS: HERALDRY, CR 55-57.
Decorations of honor	CHIVALRY: HERALDRY, CR 4501-6305.
	Decorations: HERALDRY, CR 4501-6305.
Emblems	(∅)
Emblems, National	(∅)
Escutcheons	SHIELDS: HERALDRY, CR 91-93.
Flags	FLAGS: HERALDRY, CR 101-115.
Genealogy	GENEALOGY, CS.
Hatchments	HATCHMENTS: HERALDRY, CR 41.
Insignia	INSIGNIA: ROYALTY: HERALDRY, CR 4480.
Knights and knighthood	CHIVALRY: HERALDRY, CR 4501-6305.
	Knighthood: HERALDRY, CR 4501-6305.
Military religious orders	MILITARY-RELIGIOUS ORDERS, CR 4701-4775.
Mottoes	MOTTOES: HERALDRY, CR 73-75.
Nobility	TITLES OF HONOR: HERALDRY, CR 3499-4420.
	Rank: HERALDRY, CR 3499-4420.
	Precedence: HERALDRY, CR 3499-4420.
Orders of knighthood and chivalry	ORDERS: CHIVALRY: HERALDRY, CR 4651-6305.
Precedence	TITLES OF HONOR: HERALDRY, CR 3499-4420.
	Precedence: HERALDRY, CR 3499-4420.
Seals (Numismatics)	NUMISMATICS: SEALS, CD 5041
	SEALS, CD.
Titles of honor and nobility	TITLES OF HONOR: HERALDRY, CR 3499-4420.
Visitations, Heraldic	NOBILITY: GREAT BRITAIN: GENEALOGY, CS 419.
	Armorial families: GREAT BRITIAN: GENEALOGY, CS 419
	Visitations: GREAT BRITAIN: GENEALOGY, CS 419

All of this subject headings were previously analysed in chapter four. The table shows that of the 24 subject headings four have no chain index headings. There are only 16 necessary chain index headings. There is thus a 20% overlap of the subject headings that may be removed by the chain indexing. Further the following list shows that the eight ambiguous subject headings in the group are not ambiguous as chain index headings. An ambiguous heading has already been defined as a heading with more than one classificatory reference.

AMBIGUOUS HEADINGS

Subject Headings	Chain Index Headings
Decorations of honor (CR 4501-6305; Military UB 430-435)	CHIVALRY: HERALDRY, CR 4501-6305.
Emblems (Art, N7740; Christianity, BV 150-155; Comparative religion, BL 603; Heraldry, CR: Literature, PN 6349-6358)	(∅)
Flags (Emblems of state, JC 345-7; Heraldry, CR 101-115; Merchant marine signaling, VK 385; Military science, U 360-365, UC 590-595; Naval science, V 300-305)	FLAGS: HERALDRY: CR 101-115.
Insignia (Jeweled, NK 7400-7419; Military, UC 530-535; Naval, VC 345; Royalty, CR 4480; Secret societies, HS 159-160)	INSIGNIA: ROYALTY: HERALDRY, CR 4480.
Mottoes (PN 6309-6319; Heraldry, CR 73-75)	MOTTOES: HERALDRY, CR 73-75.
Nobility (Political theory, JC 411-417; Social classes, HT 647-650)	TITLES OF HONOR: HERALDRY, CR 3499-4420.
Precedence (CR; JX 1678-9; Diplomatic, JX 4081)	TITLES OF HONOR: HERALDRY, CR 3499-4420.
Seals (Numismatics) (CD 5001-6471; National, JC 345-7)	NUMISMATICS: SEALS, CD 5041

The following list of nine redundant subject headings shows that the chain index headings no longer retain the redundancy. Redundant headings were previously defined as subject headings with the same classificatory reference.

REDUNDANT HEADINGS

Subject Headings	Chain Index Headings
Heraldry (CR)	HERALDRY, CR.
Chivalry (CR)	CHIVALRY: HERALDRY, CR 4501-6305.
Emblems (CR)	(Ø)
Knights and knighthood (CR)	CHIVALRY: HERALDRY, CR 4501-6305.
Precedence (CR)	TITLES OF HONOR: HERALDRY, CR 3499-4420.
Badges (CR 67-69)	DEVICES: HERALDRY, CR 67-69.
Devices (CR 67-69)	DEVICES: HERALDRY, CR 67-69.
Decorations of honor (CR 4501-6305)	CHIVALRY: HERALDRY, CR 4501-6305.
Orders of knighthood and chivalry (CR 4501-6305)	ORDERS: CHIVALRY: HERALDRY, CR 4651-6305.

It should be noted that not only has the redundancy been removed but also instances of incorrect and imprecise classificatory references are corrected. A third value of chain indexing may be seen in a comparison of tables of near synonyms for the heading Heraldry as previously shown in chapter four. Near synonyms are terms with the same or closely related lexical meaning. Only the *sa* headings are included in the following table.

NEAR SYNONYMS

Subject Headings	Chain Index Headings
	Class 1
Heraldry	HERALDRY, CR.
Precedence	TITLES OF HONOR: HERALDRY, CR 3499-4420.
	Class 2
Achievements (Heraldry)	(Ø)
Escutcheons	SHIELDS: HERALDRY, CR 91-93.
Hatchments	HATCHMENTS: HERALDRY, CR 41.
	Class 3
Badges	DEVICES: HERALDRY, CR 67-69.
Decorations of honor	CHIVALRY: HERALDRY, CR 4501-6305.
Devices	DEVICES: HERALDRY, CR 67-69.
Emblems	(Ø)
Emblems, National	(Ø)
Crests	CRESTS: HERALDRY, CR 55-57.
Seals (Numismatics)	NUMISMATICS: SEALS, CD 5041
Mottoes	MOTTOES: HERALDRY, CR 73-75.
Flags	FLAGS: HERALDRY, CR 101-115.

Subject Headings	Chain Index Headings
Insignia	INSIGNIA: ROYALTY: HERALDRY, CR 4480.
Orders of knighthood and chivalry	ORDERS: CHIVALRY: HERALDRY, CR 4651-6305.

Class 4

Chivalry	CHIVALRY: HERALDRY, CR 4501-6305.
Knights and knighthood	CHIVALRY: HERALDRY, CR 4501-6305.

Class 5

Nobility	TITLES OF HONOR: HERALDRY, CR 3499-4420.
Titles of honor and nobility	TITLES OF HONOR: HERALDRY, CR 3499-4420.

The near synonyms in classes 4 and 5 are completely resolved by the use of the same headings. The near synonyms of class 1, 2 and 3 are restrained by the contextual linkage in most cases.

The results of this chapter and the preceding one demonstrate that the vocabulary of the L. C. subject cataloging can be unified by chain indexing. Nearly 90% of all the class numbers treated were directly indexed. The chain index procedure produces a predictable number of sub-headings and a predictable morphologic structure for the main headings. From the Heraldry example it may be discerned that chain indexing will reduce the problems of ambiguous headings, redundant headings and near synonyms. The ambiguous headings are removed by the contextual sub-headings. The redundant headings are removed by the synonymous access headings. The near synonyms which are not access headings are isolated and controlled contextually if not lexically. Incorrect classificatory references are removed. The third hypothesis is valid. Not only can chain index headings serve as both alphabetical subject headings and classified classification headings, but chain index headings will improve the present structure of each system. Chain indexing will allow vocabulary controlled alphabetical subject access based on a classification scheme. Chain indexing will control the morphology of the system and preserve the context. Chain index headings represent the contextual extraction and unification of the vocabulary of subject cataloging.

CHAPTER VII

SUMMARY AND CONCLUSIONS

A SUMMARY OF THE ANALYSIS AND INTERPRETATION

In the test of the first hypothesis which deals with the fullness of each index each schedule of the Library of Congress classification was examined and a representative sample of the individual schedule was chosen. This sample was analysed in regard to the aspects in the sample and how those aspects were indexed. From the summary table of all 20 samples there are 731 access terms, or 44% of the 1681 schedule terms. Two hundred ninety-one class numbers or 53% of 555 class numbers are indexed; 84 Cutter numbers or 35% of 242 Cutter numbers are indexed. The total number of schedule terms appearing in identical form in the index is 263. This is 15.6% of the total of all schedule terms (1681). Two consistent patterns appeared in the analysis. First, the indexes tend to use ranges of numbers instead of single numbers. Second, the indexes tend to be fuller in regard to indexing subject subdivisions than to indexing any other subdivisions. The interpretation of these samples yielded the following results. Primarily, the indexes include more topical subdivisions than general form, geographical or chronological subdivisions. Secondly, the science and technology schedules are more fully indexed than the social sciences and humanities except for class G. Third, class numbers are more fully indexed than schedule terms. Fourth, subject subdivisions of both class and Cutter numbers are given greater indexing priority than other subdivisions. This point when considered with the third point, leads one to speculate that these indexes are some sort of specific index. Fifth, the number of schedule terms appearing in identical form in the index is very low for the humanities. There is apparently a serious lack of vocabulary control in the humanities. Sixth, class G appears to be most fully indexed in regard to identity, schedule terms, and Cutter numbers as well as being high for class numbers. The index to class G may be considered to be one of the best of the individual indexes to the Library of Congress classification. In summation, the individual indexes appear to be both inconsistent and incomplete.

In the test of the second hypothesis which deals with the relationship between subject headings and classification headings only one-fourth of the 206 subject headings tested graphemically match perfectly with both the classification and index headings. Forty percent of the classification headings are partial matches and 50% of the index headings are partial matches. The morphological-syntactical analysis applied to the first group of 49 subject headings shows a single noun in mass form to be the only recurring perfect match. Thirty-one different variants are formed by the partial matches of the first group with only two forms recurring. There are 25 discernible semantic variants in the first group. Four different inconsistencies in the classificatory references fo the first group are isolated. The Shakespeare example shows may redundant subdivisions, fifteen unused appropriate classificatory references and an inconsistent use of subsubdivisions. The combination of the results of the structural, semantic and classification tests shows only five headings or 10% of the first group pass all the tests. Only one heading in the second group of eleven headings passes all the tests. The size of the sample may tend to limit the interpretation. The vocabulary of the sample covered is only coincidentally related to the vocabulary of the classification system. Although one cannot positively state that the samples used are representative of the entire list, there is no reason to state that they are not. The investigator believes that they are representative. However the major value of this section is the success of the methodology. Examples of near synonyms, ambiguous headings and redundant headings are all isolated and defined.

Twenty-six rules for chain indexing were generated and tested in chapters five and six as the test of the third hypothesis. The chain index headings generated by these rules show 90% direct indexing and a predictable number of sub-headings. Further a predictable morphology resulted in these headings with about 84% of the main headings in the form of W or W_aW and about 95% in one of the following four forms—W, W_aW, W_aW_aW, and Proper nouns. The removal of ambiguous headings and redundant headings may also be accomplished by the application of the chain indexing rules. In addition the method of chain index headings allows the individual to reduce and isolate near synonyms as well as removing incorrect classificatory references. The chain index proves to be a more complete index than the existing L. C. indexes. It has a consistent morphology, and it retains the context of the classification on schedule in an alphabetical array.

THE DEFENSE OF THE HYPOTHESES

The first hypothesis of this study is that the indexes for individual L. C. schedules vary in fullness and do not represent a single logical development. The summary table as well as the tables for the individual samples demonstrates without a doubt that the indexes to the schedules vary in fullness. For instance, if 88% of the schedule terms for class G appear in the index, and 80% of the schedule terms for class R appear in the index, and 30% of the schedule terms for class J appear in the index, and 19% of the schedule terms for class BL-BX appear in the index, etc., then the indexes vary in fullness. Secondly, the many inconsistencies shown both in the tables in the analysis section of chapter three and in the lists in the interpretation section of that chapter make it obvious that these indexes do not result from a single logical pattern. For instance, if both class G and class J are considered to be parts of the social sciences, why is class G so well indexed and class J so poorly indexed. From the evidence presented in chapter three it is obvious that each index represents a separate development and is not necessarily consistent with the other indexes.

The second hypothesis of this study is that there is a discernible relationship demonstrating a high degree of identity between the terminology of the L. C. subject headings and the L. C. classification. Because of the limited size of the sample the hypothesis cannot be rigorously refuted. In regard to the sample, the second hypothesis is invalid. No consistent graphemic, morphological, syntactical or lexical relationship could be discerned. The only partial relationship to the classification may be found in the classificatory references and the syndetic structure. Secondly as chapter four demonstrates there is not a high degree of identity within the sample.

The third hypothesis is that the use of chain indexing will unify the vocabulary of the Library's subject cataloging so that an alphabetical array of the classification will be a list of subject headings and that a classified array of subject headings will be the classification schedule. The results of chapters five and six demonstrate the validity of this hypothesis. The vocabulary is unified as the indexability tests and morphology tests demonstrate. The example of Heraldry as well as the Shakespeare example contained in the appendix show that the chain index headings may either be in alphabetical or classified array. In fact the examples of chain index headings have appeared to be superior to the comparable subject headings or classification headings or classification index headings.

THE IMPLICATIONS OF THIS STUDY

There are eleven implications of this study resulting from the three hypotheses. One of the implications of this study is that classifiers who use the L. C. indexes sparingly, and become familiar with the individual schedules are going to be more successful than those who rely solely on the index to give them access to the schedule. Second, library school students should be taught that the indexes are inconsistent and incomplete. They must be prepared to become familiar with the schedules and not rely on the indexes. Third, it would seem justified to suggest strongly that no general index to the classification be issued if it is simply a cumulation of these individual indexes. Fourth, it is obvious that these indexes cannot be used as a tentative or initial index to a classified catalog. Fifth, students should be taught the dangers of trying to use the L. C. subject headings list as a partial index to L. C. classification. The inaccurate and imprecise classificatory references cannot be relied on. Sixth, the user of the subject headings list should be aware of the problems of near synonyms, ambiguous headings and redundant headings. Seventh, it must be acknowledged that much of the assumed context or deep structure of the L. C. subject headings is contained in both the classificatory references and the syndetic structure. This context normally disappears when the heading is applied. Eighth, the classification of a list of subject headings or descriptors should be done as the list is being developed to be consistent. As all language is classificatory, a non-classified list is controlled by this inherent classificatory property of language. Only as a classification has been defined and superimposed on a plan for developing a list of subject headings can these inherent classificatory properties of language be controlled. The nominal structure of the existing headings will only allow inherent class names of the nominal structure to create the main categories. The lexical inconsistencies of nominal classificatory language will not, cannot, allow hierarchies of any specificity to develop; they only allow categorized lists of near synonyms to result. Ninth, the chain indexing rules developed in this work follow strict structural and contextual rules in order to integrate the vocabulary of the classification schedule, the classification index, and the subject headings. The index is the subject headings; the classification schedules may be fully indexed in this fashion. This constructive approach resulting from chain indexing generates the vocabulary for subject analysis. The use of this vocabulary control is not limited to Library of Congress subject cataloging but can have implications for all classification shcemes, subject heading lists, classified catalogs, and perhaps most importantly specialized information science thesauri. Tenth, the use of the exclude list in combination with the rules allows the possibility of automatic or mechanized chain indexing. A final implication of this study is the possible uses of chain indexing to analyse a classification system. Chain indexing shows the parallel sections of a system as well as the levels of hierarchical specificity. In addition, of course, chain indexing can refine and improve the vocabulary of the classification.

THE CONCLUSION

As the first hypothesis appears to be valid, the following conclusions may be made. About half of the class numbers in L. C. classification schedules are indexed. Less than half of the schedule terms are indexed and just over a third of the Cutter numbers appearing in the schedules are indexed. If LaMontagne's figure of 1000,000 index entries is accurate,[1] and if Bead's adjustment of that figure in 1966[2] to 140,000 entries is accurate, then one may postulate that a complete specific index to the classification would contain nearly 300,000 entries. If this index were to be relative in any aspect, that is if any distributed relatives appeared, then the figure of 300,000 entries would be far too low. It may further be postulated that the Library of

Congress classification probably has at least eight times as many entries as the Library of Congress Subject Headings List. If the headings in the L. C. classification could be logically controlled by an adequate index and vocabulary control could be performed, the most complete general subject heading list would result.

In the test of the second hypothesis the investigator has found the methodology to be significant. By using the three different testing approaches may inconsistencies were isolated. The graphemic analysis sorts out areas for further structural analysis. The morphologic tests show the lack of consistent paradigmatic classes. The syntactical analysis shows an inconsistent range of structural variations. In the semantic analysis classes of near synonyms are isolated by lexical meanings while contextual meanings are found in both the classificatory references and the syndetic structure. The examination of the classificatory references shows errors, confused contextual meanings, and many unused appropriate class numbers. By applying only the examination of classificatory references to the subdivisions of Shakespeare and rearranging these subdivisions according to the classificatory references many of the same problems could be seen. Unused classificatory references could be immediately discerned. Apparent classes of near synonyms could be seen graphemically. Inconsistencies in the use of subdivisions were obvious. By the use of this method one may conclude that the vocabulary of subject headings or descriptors may be analysed graphemically, morphologically, syntactically, lexically and contextually. In addition by the graphic display of classificatory references redundant headings, ambiguous headings and near synonyms may be isolated.

The test of the third hypothesis demonstrates such a method of vocabulary control. The twenty-six rules for chain indexing provide graphemic, morphologic, syntactical, lexical and contextual control of the vocabulary of the classification. The chain index ascriptors may serve as either the classification headings or the subject headings. The index to the classification is the list of subject headings. Both subject headings and classification are organized into one vocabulary controlled system instead of two or even three systems.

SUGGESTIONS FOR FURTHER RESEARCH

This study has been most fruitful for the investigator. There are several areas for further research indicated by this paper. First, a comparison should be made fo the two published indexes to the classified catalogs using L. C. classification. How well do these indexes index the portions of the classification they are supposed to index? Second, a larger sample of subject headings should, be subjected to the forms of analysis developed in chapter three. This could be done by selecting sample headings from the names of classes and subclasses in L. C. classification. Third, the rules for chain indexing should be applied to other classification systems as a form of analysis as well as possibly generating additional rules. Certainly the notational problems of the Dewey Decimal

Classification may demand further rules for false links. Fourth, the chain index used in the *British National Bibliography* should be analysed in the light of the twenty-six rules generated in this study. Fifth, the whole problem of whether or not the classified catalog should replace the alphabetical subject catalog should be carefully discerned.

[1] *Supra,* p. 13, fn. 18.

[2] Bead, Charles C., "The Library of Congress Classification: Development, Characteristics, and Structure," in *The Use of the Library of Congress Classification, op. cit.,* p. 21.

CHAPTER VIII

LIST OF WORKS CONSULTED

Aitchison, Jean. "English Electric Company," *Classification Research Group Bulletin No. 7* in *Journal of Documentation,* XVIII (June, 1962), 80-88.

American Library Association. Resources and Technical Services Division. Cataloging and Classification Committee. "Classified Catalogs," *Library Resources & Technical Services,* VI (Summer, 1962), 274-75.

Angell, Richard S. "On the Future of the Library of Congress Classification," *Classification Research.* Proceedings of the Second International Study Conference held at Hotel Prins Hamlet, Elsinor, Denmark, 14th to 18th September, 1964. Edited by Pauline Atherton. Copenhagen: Munksgaard, 1965, Pp. 101-112.

Batty, C. D. "Chain Indexing," *Encyclopedia of Library and Information Science,* Vol. IV.

_____ . "A Documentation Training Model," *American Documentation,* XVIII (July, 1967), 125-30.

British National Bibliography. London: British National Bibliography Ltd. Council, 1950-

British Standards Institution. *Guide to the Universal Decimal Classification (UDC).* B. S. 1000C:1963. F. I. D., No. 345. London: British Standards Institution, 1963.

Brown, James Duff. *Library Classification and Cataloging.* London: Grafton & Co., 1916.

Caless, Thomas. "Preconditions of Electronic Searchability," *Reclassification, Rationale and Problems.* Proceedings of a Conference on Reclassification held at the Center of Adult Education, University of Maryland, College Park, April 4 to 6, 1968. Edited by Jean M. Perreault, General Chairman. College Park: School of Library and Infromation Sciences, 1968. Pp. 179-85.

Cardin, Clarisse. "Approach to a Bilingual Catalogue," *Canadian Library Association Bulletin,* XIII (February, 1957), 169-79.

Classification Research Group, London. *The Sayers Memorial Volume: Essays in Librarianship in Memory of William Charles Berwick Sayers.* Edited by D. J. Foskett and B. I. Palmer for the Classification Research Group. London: The Library Association, 1961.

Coates, E. J. *Subject Catalogues, Headings and Structure.* London: The Library Association, 1960.

_____ . "The Use of B. N. B. in Dictionary Cataloguing," *Library Association Record,* LIX (June, 1957), 197-202.

Collison, Robert L. *Indexes and Indexing.* A Guide to the Indexing of Books, and Collections of Books, Periodicals, Music, Gramophone Records, Films and Other Material, with a Reference Section and Suggestions for Further Reading. New York: John de Graff, Inc., 1953.

_____. *Indexing Books.* A Manual of Basic Principles. London: Ernest Benn Limited, 1962.

Cunningham, Virginia. "Library of Congress Classed Catalog for Music," *Library Resources & Technical Services,* VIII (Summer, 1964), 285-88.

Custer, Benjamin. "Editor's Introduction," Vol. I: *Dewey Decimal Classification and Relative Index.* Devised by Melvil Dewey. Edition 17. Lake Placid Club, N. Y.: Forest Press, Inc. of Lake Placid Club Education Foundation, 1965. Pp. 5-61.

Cutter, Charles A. *Rules for a Dictionary Catalog.* 4th ed., rewritten. U. S. Bureau of Education, Special Report on Public Libraries—Part II. Washington: Government Printing Office, 1904.

Daily, Jay E. "Classification and Categorization," *Encyclopedia of Library and Information Science,* Vol. 5.

_____. "The Grammar of Subject Headings, a Formulation of Rules for Subject Headings Based on a Syntactical and Morphological Analysis of the Library of Congress List." Unpublished D. L. S. dissertation, School of Library Service, Columbia University, 1957.

_____. "Many Changes, No Alterations: An Analysis of Library of Congress Subject Headings, Seventh Edition," *Library Journal,* XCII (November 1, 1967), 3961-63.

_____. "Subject Headings and the Theory of Classification," *American Documentation,* VII (October, 1957), 269-74.

Davison, Keith. *Theory of Classification.* An Examination Guidebook. London: Clive Bingley, 1966.

Dewey, H. T. "Relationships between the Headings in the Subject Catalog and the Classification Numbers of the Books," *Reclassification, Rationale and Problems.* Proceedings of a Conference on Reclassification held at the Center of Adult Education, University of Maryland, College Park, April 4 to 6, 1968. Edited by Jean M. Perreault, General Chairman. College Park: School of Library and Information Sciences, 1968. Pp. 57-78.

_____. "Some Aspects of the Classified Catalog," *The Subject Analysis of Library Materials.* Papers presented at an Institute, June 24-28, 1952, under the sponsorship of the School of Library Service, Columbia University, and the A. L. A. Division of Cataloging and Classification. Edited, with an introduction by Maurice Tauber. New York: School of Library Service, Columbia University, 1953. Pp. 114-29.

Dewey, Melvil. "Melvil Dewey's Introduction," Vol. I: *Dewey Decimal Classification and Relative Index.* Devised by Melvil Dewey. Edition 17. Lake Placid Club, N.Y.: Forest Press, Inc. of Lake Placid Club Education Foundation, 1965. Pp. 63-108.

Doughty, D. W. "Chain Procedure Subject Indexing and Featuring a Classified Catalogue," *Library Association Record,* LVII (May, 1955), 173-78.

Doyle, Irene M. "Library of Congress Classification for the Academic Library," *The Role of Calssification in the Modern American Library.* Papers presented at an Institute conducted by the University of Illinois Graduate School of Library Science, November 1-4, 1959. Champaign, Ill.: Illini Union Bookstore, 1959. Pp. 76-92.

Dunkin, Paul S. *Cataloging U. S. A.* Chicago: American Library Association, 1969.

Elrod, J. McRee. "Classed Catalog in the Fifties," *Library Resources & Technical Services,* V (Spring, 1961), 142-56.

_____. "Korean Classified Catalog," *Library Resources & Technical Services,* IV (Fall, 1960), 331-36.

Farradane, J. "The Challenge of Information Retrieval," *Journal of Documentation,* XVII (December, 1961), 233-44.

_____. "Fundamental Fallacies and New Need in Classification," *The Sayers Memorial Volume: Essays in Librarianship in Memory of William Charles Berwick Sayers.* Edited by D. J. Foskett and B. I. Palmer for the Classification Research Group. London: The Library Association, 1961. Pp. 120-35.

_____. "A Scientific Theory of Classification and Indexing," *Journal of Documentation,* VI (1950), 83-99, VIII (1952), 73-92.

Fielding, D. "Structure of the Classified Catalogue," *Australian Library Journal,* XII (Summer, 1963), 154-58.

Foskett, D. J. "Catalogue and Reference Service," *Librarian and Book World,* XLI (November, 1952), 213-18.

_____. *Classification and Indexing in the Social Sciences.* Washington: Butterworths, 1963.

_____. "Two Notes on Indexing Techniques," *Journal of Documentation,* XVIII (December, 1962), 188-92.

Frarey, Carlyle J. "Subject Headings," Vol. 1, part 2: *The State of the Library Art,* edited by Ralph R. Shaw. New Brunswick, N.J.: Graduate School of Library Service, Rutgers, The State University, 1960.

Freeman, C. B. "Classified Catalogue, Plea for its Abolition in Public Libraries," *Library Review,* no. 146, (Summer, 1963), 93-98.

Gleason, H. A. *An Introduction to Descriptive Linguistics.* Rev. ed. New York: Holt, Rinehart and Winston, 1961.

Gull, C. D. "Some Remarks on Subject Headings," *Special Libraries,* XL (March, 1949), 83-88.

Hanson, J. C. M. "The Library of Congress and its New Catalog: Some Unwritten History," *Essays Offered to Herbert Putnam by his Colleagues and Friends on his Thirtieth Anniversary as Librarian of Congress: 5 April 1929.* Edited by William Warner Bishop and Andrew Keogh. New Haven: Yale University Press, 1929. Pp. 178-94.

_____. "Library of Congress Classification for College Libraries," *Library Journal,* XLVI (February 15, 1921), 151-54.

Hardy, May G. "The Library of Congress Subject Catalog: An Evaluation," *Library Quarterly,* XXII (January, 1952), 40-50.

Haykin, David Judson. *Subject Headings, A Practical Guide.* Washington: Government Printing Office, 1951.

Henkle, Herman H. "The Classified Catalogue as an Aid to Research," *The Role of Classification in the Modern American Library.* Papers presented at an Institute conducted by the University of Illinois Graduate School of Library Science, November 1-4, 1959. Champaign, Ill.: Illini Union Bookstore, 1959. Pp. 42-52.

_____. "Some Unanswered Questions," *Library Quarterly,* XXVI (October, 1956), 348-55.

Herrick, Mary Darrah. "Classified Catalog at Boston University, 1948-1964," *Library Resources & Technical Services,* VIII (Summer, 1964), 289-99.

_____. "Development of a Classified Catalog for a University Library," *College & Research Libraries,* XIV (October, 1953), 418-24.

Hicks, Frederick C. "Library of Congress Classification and its Printed Catalog Cards," *Library Journal,* XXXI (June, 1906), 255-56.

Hines, Theodore C. "Revolution in Public Library Cataloging," *Library Journal,* LXXXVII (May 1, 1962), 1725-28.

Hoage, A. Annette Lewis. "The Library of Congress Classification in the United States: A Survey of Opinions and Practices, with Attention to Problems of Structure and Application." Unpublished D. L. S. dissertation, School of Library Service, Columbia University, 1961.

Hulme, E. Wyndham. "On the Construction of the Subject Catalogue in Scientific and Technical Libraries," *Library Association Record,* III (October, 1901), 507-13.

_____. "Principles of Book Classification," *Readings in Library Cataloguing.* Edited and introduced by R. K. Oldings.. Hamden, Conn.: Shoe String Press, 1966. Pp. 108-140.

Immroth, John Phillip. *A Guide to Library of Congress Classification.* Library Science Text Series. Rochester, N. Y.: Libraries Unlimited, 1968.

International Federation for Documentation. *Proceedings of the International Study Conference on Classification for Information Retrieval,* held at Beatrice Webb House, Dorking, England, 13th-17th May 1957. London: ASLIB: New York: Pergamon Press, 1957.

Jacobs, Roderick A. and Peter S. Rosenbaum. *English Transformational Grammar.* With an Epilogue by Paul M. Postal. A Blaisdell Book in the Humanities. Waltham, Mass.: Blaisdell Publishing Company, 1968.

Jolley, L. *The Principles of Cataloguing.* With a foreword by R. O. MacKenna. New York: Philosophical Library, 1960.

Jonker, Frederick. *Indexing Theory, Indexing Methods and Search Devices.* New York: The Scarecrow Press, Inc., 1964.

Kaiser, Julius Otto. "Systematic Indexing." *Readings in Library Cataloguing,* edited and introduced by R. K. Olding. Hamden, Conn.: The Shoe String Press, Inc., 1966. Pp. 145-162.

Kennedy, R. F. *Classified Cataloguing, A Practical Guide.* Cape Town: A. A. Balkema, 1966.

Kent, Allen. *Textbook on Mechanized Information Retrieval.* 2d ed. Library Science and Documentation, A Series of Texts and Monographs, Vol. III. New York: Interscience Publishers, 1966.

LaMontagne, Leo F. *American Library Classification with Special Reference to the Library of Congress.* Hamden, Conn.: Shoe String Press, 1961.

Langridge, Derek. "Classification and Book Indexing," *The Sayers Memorial Volume: Essays in Librarianship in Memory of William Charles Berwick Sayers.* Edited by D. J. Foskett and B. I. Palmer for the Classification Research Group. London: The Library Association, 1961. Pp. 182-193.

Lilley, Oliver L. "Evaluation of the Subject Catalog," *American Documentation,* V (1954), 41-60.

_____. "Terminology, Form, Specificity and the Syndetic Structure of Subject Headings for English Literature." Unpublished D. L. S. dissertation, School of Library Service, Columbia University, 1958.

Line, Maurice B. "Classified Catalogue of Musical Scores: Some Problems," *Library Association Record,* LIV (November 1952), 362-64.

Lynn, Jeannette M. and Zola Hilton. "A Code for the Construction and Maintenance of the Classified Catalogue," *The Classified Catalog, Basic Principles and Practices,* by Jesse H. Shera and Margaret Egan. Chicago: American Library Association, 1956. Pp. 64-103.

MacCallum Walker, T. "The Subject-Approach in the University Library," *Libri,* VI (1956), 255-70.

Mann, Margaret. *Introduction to Cataloging and the Classification of Books.* 2d ed. Chicago: American Library Association, 1943.

Martel, Chalres. "Classification," *Report of the Librarian of Congress,* and Report of the Superintendent of the Library Buildings and Grounds for the fiscal year ending June 30, 1911. Washington: Government Printing Office, 1911. Pp. 58-64.

_____. "Classification: a Brief Coinspectus of Present Day Library Practice," *Library Journal,* XXXVI (August, 1911), 410-16.

_____. ""Library of Congress Classification," *ALA Bulletin,* V (July, 1911), 230-32.

_____. "The Library of Congress Classification," *Essays Offered to Herbert Putnam by his Colleagues and Firends on his Thirtieth Anniversary as Librarian of Congress: 5 April 1929.* Edited by William Warner Bishop and Andrew Keogh. New Haven: Yale University Press, 1929. Pp. 327-32.

Maryland. University. School of Library and Information Services. *Reclassification, Rationale and Problems.* Proceedings of a Conference on Reclassification held at the Center of Adult Education, University of

Maryland, College Park, April 4 to 6, 1968. Edited by Jean M. Perreault, General Chairman. Conference Proceedings from the School of Library and Information Services, University of Maryland, Vol. 1. College Park: School of Library and Information Services, 1968.

Metcalfe, John. *Alphabetical Subject Indication of Information.* Rutgers Series on Systems for the Intellectual Organization of Information, Vol. III. New Brunswick, N. J.: Graduate School of Library Service, Rutgers, the State University, 1965.

_____. *Information Indexing and Subject Cataloguing, Alphabetical: Classified, Coordinate: Mechanical.* New York: The Scarecrow Press, Inc., 1957.

_____. *Subject Classifying and Indexing of Libraries and Literature.* New York: The Scarecrow Press, Inc., 1959.

Mills, J. "Chain Indexing and the Classified Catalogue." *Library Association Record,* LVII (April, 1955), 141-48.

_____. "Indexing a Classification Scheme," *Indexer,* II (Autumn, 1960), 40-48.

_____. *A Modern Outline of Library Classification.* London: Chapman & Hall, 1960.

Needham, C. D. *Organizing Knowledge in Libraries: An Introduction to Classification and Cataloging.* London: Andre Deutsch, 1965.

Palmer, Bernard I. and A. J. Wells. *The Fundamentals of Library Classification.* London: George Allen & Unwin Ltd., 1951.

Perley, Clarence W. "Recent Developments in the Library of Congress Classification," *Proceedings of the Catalog Section,* American Library Association, Washington, D. C., Conference May 13-18, 1929. Chicago: Catalog Section, American Library Association, 1929.

Perreault, Jean M. "Categories and Relators: A New Schema," *Revue de Internationale Documentation,* XXXII (1965), 136-44.

_____. "Documentary Relevance and Structural Hierarchy," *American Documentation,* XVII (July, 1966), 1936-39.

_____. "A New Device for Achieving Hospitality in Array." *American Documentation,* XVI (July, 1965), 245-46.

_____. "On Bibliography and Automation: or, How to Reinvent the Catalog," *Libri,* XV (1965), 287-338.

_____. *Re-Classification: Some Warnings and a Proposal.* Illinois. University. Graduate School of Library Science. *Occasional Papers,* no. 87, Sept. 1967. Urbana: University of Illinois Graduate School of Library Service, 1967.

Perry, J. W. and Allen Kent. *Tools for Machine Literature Searching.* New York: Interscience Publishers, 1958.

Pettee, Julia. "The Philosophy of Subject Headings," *Special Libraries,* XXIII (April, 1932), 181-82.

_____. *Subject Headings, the History and Theory of the Alphabetical Subject Approach to Books.* New York: The H. W. Wilson Co., 1946.

Pettus, Clyde. *Subject Headings in Education: A systematic List for Use in a Dictionary Catalog.* With a preface by Margaret Mann. New York: The H. W. Wilson Co., 1938.

Phillips, W. Howard. *A Primer of Book Classification.* 5th ed. London: Association of Assistant Librarians, 1961.

Prevost, Marie. "An Approach to Theory and Method in General Subject Heading," *Library Quarterly,* XVI (1946), 140-51.

Ranganathan, S. R. *Classified Catalogue Code with Additional Rules for Dictionary Catalogue Code.* Assisted by A. Neelameghan. New York: Asia Publishing House, 1964.

_____. *Colon Classification.* Ranganathan Series in Library Science, 4; Madras Library Association Publishing Series, 26 New York: Asia Publishing House, 1963.

_____. *Dictionary Catalogue Code.* Madras Library Association Publication Series, 14. Madras: Thompson: London: Grafton, 1945.

_____. *Theory of Library Catalogue.* Madras: Madras Library Association, 1938.

Reid, A. S. "Occupational Safety and Health," *Classification Research Group Bulletin No. 7* in *Journal of Documentation,* XVIII (June, 1962), 66-69.

Richmond, Phyllis A. "Cats: an Example of Concealed Classification in Subject Headings," *Library Resources & Technical Services,* III (Spring, 1959), 102-112.

_____. "General Advantages and Disadvantages of Using the Library of Congress Classification," *The Use of the Library of Congress Classification.* Proceedings of the Institute on the Use of the Library of Congress Classification, Sponsored by the American Library Association, Resources and Technical Services Division, Cataloging and Classification Section, New York City, July 7-9, 1966. Edited by Richard H. Schimmelpfeng and C. Donald Cook. Chicago: American Library Association, 1968. Pp. 209-20.

Roberts, M. A. *The Library of Congress in Relation to Research.* Washington: Government Printing Office, 1939.

Robertson, David Allen. "The L.C. Classification as an Aid to Research," *Proceedings of the Catalog Section,* American Library Association, Washington, D. C., Conference May 13-18, 1929. Chicago: Catalog Section, American Library Association, 1929.

Sahaya, S. "Library of Congress and its Classification," *Modern Librarian,* XV (1945), 82-86.

Savage, Ernest Albert. *Manual of Book Classification and Display for Public Libraries.* London: Allen & Unwin and the Library Association, 1946.

Sayers, W. C. Berwick. *Canons of Classification, Applied to "The Subject," "The Expansive," "The Decimal," and "The Library of Congress" Classifications· A Study of Bibliographical Classification Method.* London: Grafton, 1915.

_____. *An Introduction to Library Classification· Theoretical, Historical and Practical* with readings, exercises and examination papers. 9th ed. London: Grafton, 1958.

_____. *A Manual of Classification for Librarians and Bibliographers.* 3d ed., rev. London: Andre Deutsch, 1959.

Scheerer, George. "Subject Catalog Examined," *Library Quarterly,* XXVII (July, 1957), 187-98.

Schimmelpfeng, Richard H. and C. Donald Cook, eds. *The Use of the Library of Congress Classification.* Proceedings of the Institute on the Use of the Library of Congress Classification, Sponsored by the American Library Association, Resources and Technical Services Division, Cataloging and Classification Section, New York City, July 7-9, 1966. Chicago: American Library Association, 1968.

Schwartz, Jacob. "A Dozen Desultory Denunciations of the Dictionary Catalogue, with a Theory of Cataloguing," *Library Journal,* IX (December, 1886), 470-74.

Sharp, John R. *Some Fundamentals of Information Retrieval.* New York: London House & Maxwell, 1965.

Shera, Jesse H. and Margaret Egan. *The Classified Catalog, Basic Principles and Practices.* With a Code for the Construction and Maintenance of the Classified Catalog, by Jeannette M. Lynn and Zola Hilton. Chicago: American Library Association, 1956.

Smither, Reginald Ernest. "Library of Congress Classification," *Library World,* XVI (November, 1913), 130-36.

Surramaniam, D. "Evolution of Classified Catalogue," *Indian Librarian,* IX (June, 1954), 17-21.

Swank, Raynard. "Subject Catalogs, Classifications, or Bibliographies? A Review of Critical Discussions, 1876-1942," *Library Quarterly,* XIV (October, 1944), 316-32.

Tandon, Umesh Chandra. "Alphabetisation in Classified Catalogue," *Herald of Library Science,* IV (April, 1965), 167-68.

Tauber, Maurice F. and Edith Wise. *Classification Systems.* Vol. 1, part 3: *The State of Library Art.* Edited by Ralph R. Shaw. New Brunswick, N.J.: Graduate School of Library Science, Rutgers, The State University, 1961. Pp. 140-188.

Tauber, Maurice, ed. *The Subject Analysis of Library Materials.* Papers presented at an Institute, June 24-28, 1952, under the sponsorship of the School of Library Service, Columbia University, and the A.L.A. Division of Cataloging and Classification. Edited, with an introduction by Maurice Tauber. New York: School of Library Service, Columbia University, 1953.

Tauber, Maurice F. *Technical Services in Libraries.* New York: Columbia University Press, 1953.

Taylor, Archer. *General Subject-Indexes since 1548.* Philadelphia: University of Pennsylvania Press, 1966.

Taylor, Desmond. "Reclassification to LC: Planning and Personnel," *Reclassification, Rationale and Problems.* Proceedings of a Conference on Recalssification held at the Center of Adult Education, University of Maryland, College Park, April 4 to 6, 1968. Edited by Jean M. Perreault, General Chairman. College Park: School of Library and INformation Sciences, 1968. Pp. 97-115.

Taylor, K. L. "Subject Catalogs vs. Classified Catalogs," *The Subject Analysis of Library Materials.* Papers presented at an Institue, June 24-28, 1952, under the sponsorship of the School of Library Service, Columbia University, and the A.L.A. Division of Cataloging and Classification. Edited, with an introduction by Maurice Tauber. New York School of Library Service, Columbia University, 1953. Pp. 100-13.

Thirumalaimuthuswamy, A. "Entries in a Classified Catalog," *Indian Librarian,* XIX (Summer, 1964), 75-82.

Thompson, Anthony. "Rules for Subject Headings, Periodicals, Subject Index, Royal Institute of British Architects Library," *Journal of Documentation,* IX (September, 1953), 69-74.

U. S. Library of Congress. *Annual Report of the Librarian of Congress.* Washington: Government Printing Office, 1901-

_____. *The Library of Congress and its Activities.* Washington: Government Printing Office, 1926.

_____. *The Library of Congress and its Work.* Washington: Government Printing Office, 1907.

_____. Subject Cataloging Division. *Departmental and Divisional Manuals,* No. 3. Washington: Library of Congress, 1950.

Venkatesan, P. "Classified Catalogue, its Components and Characteristics," *Library Herald,* VII (January, 1965), 235-48.

Vickery, B. C. *Classification and Indexing in Science.* With an introduction by D. J. Foskett. 2d ed. (enl.) London: Butterworths, 1959.

Wilson, M. "Library of Congress Classification," *Australian Institute of Librarians Proceedings,* II (1939), 113-17.

Wilson, Tom. "Chain Indexing Is Not Mysterious," *Library Journal,* LXXXVIII (January 15, 1963), 189-90.

Yerke, T. B. and C. M. Walker. "Oxford System: A Study of its Uses at a Forest Experiment Station," *Journal of Forestry,* LXI (April, 1963), 295-96.

APPENDIX

THE SHAKESPEARE CHAIN INDEX

The entire chain index for Shakespeare, PR 2750-3112, is given here. First the index is given in alphabetical format. Second all feature headings or feature cards are displayed in a classified fashion.

The analysis and interpretation of this index is contained in chapter five of this study.

SHAKESPEARE CHAIN INDEX
ALPHABETICAL ARRAY

ACTORS: SHAKESPEARE, PR 3112.
Adaptations: SHAKESPEARE, PR 2877-2879.
Addresses: BIOGRAPHY: SHAKESPEARE, PR 2899.
AFRICAN TRANSLATIONS: SHAKESPEARE, PR 2798.
The age of Shakespeare, PR 2910.
ALL'S WELL THAT ENDS WELL: FACSIMILES: QUARTOS: SHAKESPEARE, PR 2750.B1.
ALL'S WELL THAT ENDS WELL: ORIGINAL EDITIONS: QUARTOS: SHAKESPEARE, PR 2750.A1.
ALL'S WELL THAT ENDS WELL: SHAKESPEARE, PR 2801.
ALLUSIONS: AUTHORSHIP: SHAKESPEARE, PR 2959.
ALLUSIONS: BIOGRAPHY: SHAKESPEARE, PR 2909.
ALMANACS: SELECTIONS: SHAKESPEARE, PR 2770-2771.
AMERICAN BACONIAN THEORY: AUTHORSHIP CONTROVERSY: SHAKESPEARE, PR 2945.
AMERICAN DRAMATIC REPRESENTATIONS: SHAKESPEARE, PR 3105
AMERICAN INDIAN TRANSLATIONS: SHAKESPEARE, PR 2799.
AMERICAN SOCIETIES: SHAKESPEARE, PR 2887.
Ancestry: BIOGRAPHY: SHAKESPEARE, PR 2901.
ANNIVERSARIES: SHAKESPEARE, PR 2923.
Annotated editions: COLLECTED WORKS: SHAKESPEARE, PR 2752-2754.
Anthologies: POEMS: FACSIMILES: QUARTOS: SHAKESPEARE, PR 2750.B42.
Anthologies: POEMS: ORIGINAL EDITIONS: QUARTOS: SHAKESPEARE, PR 2750.A42.
Anthologies: POEMS: SHAKESPEARE, PR 2942.
Anthologies: SHAKESEPARE, PR 2767-2771.
ANTONY AND CLEOPATRA: FACSIMILES: QUARTOS: SHAKESPEARE, PR 2750.B2.
ANTONY AND CLEOPATRA: ORIGINAL EDITIONS: QUARTOS: SHAKESPEARE, PR 2750.A2.
ANTONY AND CLEOPATRA: SHAKESPEARE, PR 2802.

ARCHERY: TREATMENT: SHAKESPEARE, PR 3069.A6.
ARDEN OF FEVERSHAM: SPURIOUS WORKS: FACSIMILES: QUARTOS:
SHAKESPEARE, PR 2750.B54.
ARDEN OF FEVERSHAM: SPURIOUS WORKS: ORIGINAL EDITIONS:
QUARTOS: SHAKESPEARE, PR 2750.A54.
ARDEN OF FEVERSHAM: SPURIOUS WORKS: SHAKESPEARE, PR 2854.
ARRAIGNMENT OF PARIS: SPURIOUS WORKS: FACSIMILES: QUARTOS:
SHAKESPEARE, PR 2750.B55.
ARRAIGNMENT OF PARIS: SPURIOUS WORKS: ORIGINAL EDITIONS:
QUARTOS: SHAKESPEARE, PR 2750.A55.
ARRAIGNMENT OF PARIS: SPURIOUS WORKS: SHAKESPEARE, PR 2855.
ART: TREATMENT: SHAKESPEARE, PR 3034.
ARTIFICIAL LANGUAGE TRANSLATIONS: SHAKESPEARE, PR 2800.
AS YOU LIKE IT: FACSIMILES: QUARTOS: SHAKESPEARE, PR 2750.B3.
AS YOU LIKE IT: ORIGINAL EDITIONS: QUARTOS: SHAKESPEARE,
PR 2750.A3.
AS YOU LIKE IT: SHAKESPEARE, PR 2803.
ASIAN TRANSLATIONS: SHAKESPEARE, PR 2796.
Astrology: TREATMENT: SHAKESPEARE, PR 3053.
ASTRONOMY: TREATMENT: SHAKESPEARE, PR 3053.
AUTHORSHIP CONTROVERSY: SHAKESPEARE, PR 2939-2948.
AUTHORSHIP: SHAKESPEARE, PR 2937-2961.
Bacon-Shakespeare controversy, PR 2941-2948.
BACONIAN THEORY: AUTHORSHIP CONTROVERSY: SHAKESPEARE,
PR 2941-2946.
BEAUMONT AND FLETCHER: AUTHORSHIP: SHAKESPEARE, PR 2958.B4.
BIBLE: TREATMENT: SHAKESPEARE, PR 3012.
Bibliography: SHAKESPEARE, *USE* Z8811-8813.
BIOGRAPHY: SHAKESPEARE, PR 2885-2935.
BIRTH OF MERLIN: SPURIOUS WORKS: FACSIMILES: QUARTOS:
SHAKESPEARE, PR 2750.B56.
BIRTH OF MERLIN: SPURIOUS WORKS: ORIGINAL EDITIONS: QUARTOS:
SHAKESPEARE, PR 2750.A56.
BIRTH OF MERLIN: SPURIOUS WORKS: SHAKESPEARE, PR 2856.
Birthday books: SELECTIONS: SHAKESPEARE, PR 2770-2771.
BOTANY: TREATMENT: SHAKESPEARE, PR 3041.
BOTTOM THE WEAVER: SPURIOUS WORKS: FACSIMILES:
QUARTOS: SHAKESPEARE, PR 2750.B57
BOTTOM THE WEAVER: SPURIOUS WORKS: ORIGINAL EDITIONS:
QUARTOS: SHAKESPEARE, PR 2750.A57.
BOTTOM THE WEAVER: SPURIOUS WORKS: SHAKESPEARE, PR 2857.
BRITISH DRAMATIC REPRESENTATIONS: SHAKESPEARE, PR 3106.
British literature, PR.
British societies: SHAKESPEARE, PR 2888.
Celebrations: SHAKESPEARE, PR 2923.
CHARACTERS: CRITICISM: SHAKESPEARE, PR 2989-2993.

CHEMISTRY: TREATMENT: SHAKESPEARE, PR 3059.
CHRONOLOGY: AUTHORSHIP: SHAKESPEARE, PR 2961.
Classics: TREATMENT: SHAKESPEARE, PR 3037.
Collations: FOLIOS: SHAKESPEARE, PR 2751 (.A6-Z) *USE* Z 8811-8813.
Collected essays: BIOGRAPHY: SHAKESPEARE, PR 2890.
COLLECTED POEMS: FACSIMILES: QUARTOS: SHAKESPEARE, PR 2750.B41.
COLLECTED POEMS: ORIGINAL EDITIONS: QUARTOS: SHAKESPEARE,
    PR 2750.A41.
COLLECTED POEMS: SHAKESPEARE, PR 2841.
COLLECTED PAPERS: BIOGRAPHY: SHAKESPEARE, PR 2890.
COLLECTED PARAPHRASES: SHAKESPEARE, PR 2877.
COLLECTED REPRINTS: QUARTOS: SHAKESPEARE, PR 2750.C1-C9.
COLLECTED WORKS: SHAKESPEARE, PR 2751-2754.
COLLECTED WORKS: SPURIOUS WORKS: FACSIMILES: QUARTOS:
    SHAKESPEARE, PR 2750.B51.
COLLECTED WORKS: SPURIOUS WORKS: ORIGINAL EDITIONS: QUARTOS:
    SHAKESPEARE, PR 2750.A51.
COLLECTED WORKS: SPURIOUS WORKS: SHAKESPEARE, PR 2851.
COLLIER CONTROVERSY: MANUSCRIPTS: SHAKESPEARE, PR 2951.
COMEDIES: CRITICISM: SHAKESPEARE, PR 2981.
COMEDIES: SELECTED WORKS: SHAKESPEARE, PR 2761.
COMEDY OF ERRORS: FACSIMILES: QUARTOS: SHAKESPEARE,
    PR 2750.B4.
COMEDY OF ERRORS: ORIGINAL EDITIONS: QUARTOS: SHAKESPEARE,
    PR 2750.A4.
COMEDY OF ERRORS: SHAKESPEARE, PR 2804.
COMMENTARIES: COLLECTED WORKS: SHAKESPEARE, PR 2752-2754.
COMPARATIVE STUDIES: TRANSLATIONS: SHAKESPEARE, PR 2881.
COMPREHENSIVE TREATIES: BIOGRAPHY: SHAKESPEARE, PR 2894-2900.
CONCORDANCES: SHAKESPEARE, PR 2892.
CONTEMPORARIES: AUTHORSHIP: SHAKESPEARE, PR 2957-2958.
CONTEMPORARIES: BIOGRAPHY: SHAKESPEARE, PR 2911-2913.
CORIOLANUS: FACSIMILES: QUARTOS: SHAKESPEARE, PR 2750.B5.
CORIOLANUS: ORIGINAL EDITIONS: QUARTOS: SHAKESPEARE,
    PR 2750.A5.
CORIOLANUS: SHAKESPEARE, PR 2805.
CORPUS HAMLETICUM: SHAKESPEARE, PR 2807.A7.
CRAFTS: TREATMENT: SHAKESPEARE, PR 3036.
CRIME: TREATMENT: SHAKESPEARE, PR 3026.
Criminals: TREATMENT: SHAKESPEARE, PR 3026.
Criticism: Individual works *SEE* Title of Individual work.
CRITICISM: SHAKESPEARE, PR 2965-3088.
Criticism: SHAKESPEARE, PR 2885-2935.
CRITICISM: SPURIOUS WORKS: SHAKESPEARE, PR 2875.
CYMBELINE: FACSIMILES: QUARTOS: SHAKESPEARE, PR 2750.B6
CYMBELINE: ORIGINAL EDITIONS: QUARTOS: SHAKESPEARE, PR 2750.A6.
CYMBELINE: SHAKESPEARE, PR 2806.

DANISH TRANSLATIONS: SHAKESPEARE, PR 2787-2788.
Death: BIOGRAPHY: SHAKESPEARE, PR 2908.
Descriptive bibliography: FOLOIS: SHAKESPEARE, PR 2751 (.A6-Z) *USE* Z8811-8813.
DIALECT: SHAKESPEARE, PR 3088.
Dictionaries: LANGUAGE: SHAKESPEARE, PR (3073) *USE* PR 2892.
Dictionaries: SHAKESPEARE, PR 2892.
DOUBLE FALSEHOOD: SPURIOUS WORKS: FACSIMILES: QUARTOS: SHAKESPEARE, PR 2750.B58.
DOUBLE FALSEHOOD: SPURIOUS WORKS: ORIGINAL EDITIONS: QUARTOS: SHAKESPEARE, PR 2750.A58.
DOUBLE FALSEHOOD: SPURIOUS WORKS: SHAKESPEARE, PR 2858.
Doubtful works: FACSIMILES: QUARTOS: SHAKESPEARE, PR 2750.B51-B73.
Doubtful works: ORIGINAL EDITIONS: QUARTOS: SHAKESPEARE, PR 2750.A51-A73.
Doubtful works: SHAKESPEARE, PR 2851-2875.
Drama: BIOGRAPHY: SHAKESPEARE, PR 2935.
DRAMA: ENGLISH LITERATURE, PR 2411-3195.
Dramatic art: CRITICISM: SHAKESPEARE, PR 2995-2997.
DRAMATIC REPRESENTATIONS: SHAKESPEARE, PR 3091-3112.
Dramaturgy: CRITICISM: SHAKESPEARE, PR 2995-2997.
DUTCH COMPREHENSIVE TREATISES: BIOGRAPHY: SHAKESPEARE, PR 2898.D8.
DUTCH DRAMATIC REPRESENTATIONS: SHAKESPEARE, PR 3092.D8.
DUTCH TRANSLATIONS: SHAKESPEARE, PR 2775-2776.
DUTCH TREATISES: CRITICISM: SHAKESPEARE, PR 2979.D8.
ECONOMICS: TREATMENT: SHAKESPEARE, PR 3021.
Education: BIOGRAPHY: SHAKESPEARE, PR 2903.
EDUCATION: TREATMENT: SHAKESPEARE, PR 3031.
EDWARD III: SPURIOUS WORKS: FACSIMILES: QUARTOS: SHAKESPEARE, PR 2750.B59.
EDWARD III: SPURIOUS WORKS: ORIGINAL EDITIONS: QUARTOS: SHAKESPEARE, PR 2750.A59.
EDWARD III: SPURIOUS WORKS: SHAKESPEARE, PR 2859.
ELIZABETHAN ENGLAND: BIOGRAPHY: SHAKESPEARE, PR 2910.
ENGLISH BACONIAN THEORY: AUTHORSHIP CONTROVERSY: SHAKESPEARE, PR 2944.
ENGLISH COMPREHENSIVE TREATISES: BIOGRAPHY: SHAKESPEARE, PR 2894-2895.
ENGLISH CONTEMPORARIES: BIOGRAPHY: SHAKESPEARE, PR 2912.
ENGLISH DRAMATIC REPRESENTATIONS: SHAKESPEARE, PR 3091.
ENGLISH LITERATURE, PR.
ENGLISH SOCIETIES: SHAKESPEARE, PR 2888.
ENGLISH TREATISES: CRITICISM: SHAKESPEARE, PR 2975-2976.
ESPERANTO TRANSLATIONS: SHAKESPEARE, PR 2800.E7.
Esthetics: CRITICISM: SHAKESPEARE, PR 2986.

ETHICS: TREATMENT: SHAKESPEARE, PR 3007.
EUROPEAN TRANSLATIONS: SHAKESPEARE, PR 2775-2795.
Extracts: SPURIOUS WORKS: FACSIMILES: QUARTOS: SHAKESPEARE, PR 2750.B52.
Extracts: SPURIOUS WORKS: ORIGINAL EDITIONS: QUARTOS: SHAKESPEARE, PR 2750.A52.
Extracts: SPURIOUS WORKS: SHAKESPEARE, PR 2852.
FACSIMILES: FIRST FOLIO: SHAKESPEARE, PR 2751.A15.
FACSIMILES: FOLIOS: SHAKESPEARE, PR 2751.
FACSIMILES: FOURTH FOLIO: SHAKESPEARE, PR 2751.A45.
FACSIMILES: QUARTOS: SHAKESPEARE, PR 2750.B1-B73.
FACSIMILES: SECOND FOLIO: SHAKESPEARE, PR 2751.A25.
FACSIMILES: THIRD FOLIO: SHAKESPEARE, PR 2751.A35.
FAIR EM: SPURIOUS WORKS: FACSIMILES: QUARTOS: SHAKESPEARE, PR 2750.B60.
FAIR EM: SPURIOUS WORKS: ORIGINAL EDITIONS: QUARTOS: SHAKESPEARE, PR 2750.A60.
FAIR EM: SPURIOUS WORKS: SHAKESPEARE, PR 2860.
FALSTAFF: CRITICISM: SHAKESPEARE, PR 2993.F2.
FAMILY: BIOGRAPHY: SHAKESPEARE, PR 2901.
FEMALE CHARACTERS: CRITICISM: SHAKESPEARE, PR 2991.
FICTION: BIOGRAPHY: SHAKESPEARE, PR 2935.
FIFTH OF NOVEMBER: SPURIOUS WORKS: FACSIMILES: QUARTOS: SHAKESPEARE, PR 2750.B61.
FIFTH OF NOVEMBER: SPURIOUS WORKS: ORIGINAL EDITIONS: QUARTOS: SHAKESPEARE, PR 2750.A61.
FIFTH OF NOVEMBER: SPURIOUS WORKS: SHAKESPEARE, PR 2861.
FIRST FOLIO: SHAKESPEARE, PR 2751.A1.
Fletcher and Beaumont; AUTHORSHIP: SHAKESPEARE, PR 2958.B4.
FOLIOS: SHAKESPEARE, PR 2751.
Folk-lore: TREATMENT: SHAKESPEARE, PR 3004.
Foreign countries: BIOGRAPHY: SHAKESPEARE, PR (2936) *USE* PR 2971.
FOREIGN SOURCES: SHAKESPEARE, PR 2954.
FORERUNNERS: AUTHORSHIP: SHAKESPEARE, PR 2956.
FOURTH FOLIO: SHAKESPEARE, PR 2751.A4.
France: BIOGRAPHY: SHAKESPEARE, PR (2936) *USE* PR 2971.
FRANCE: CRITICISM: SHAKESPEARE, PR 2971.F7.
FRENCH COMPREHENSIVE TREATISES: BIOGRAPHY: SHAKESPEARE, PR 2896.
FRENCH CONTEMPORARIES: BIOGRAPHY: SHAKESPEARE, PR 2913.
FRENCH DRAMATIC REPRESENTATIONS: SHAKESPEARE, PR 3107.
FRENCH SOCIETIES: SHAKESPEARE, PR 2889.
FRENCH TRANSLATIONS: SHAKESPEARE, PR 2777-2779.
FRENCH TREATISES: CRITICISM: SHAKESPEARE, PR 2977.
FURNESS, HORACE HOWARD: SCHOLARS: CRITICISM: SHAKESPEARE, PR 2972.F7.

Geography: TREATMENT: SHAKESPEARE, PR 3014.
GERMAN COMPREHENSIVE TREATISES: BIOGRAPHY: SHAKESPEARE,
   PR 2897.
GERMAN DRAMATIC REPRESENTATIONS: SHAKESPEARE, PR 3108.
GERMAN TRANSLATIONS: SHAKESPEARE, PR 2780-2782.
GERMAN TREATISES: CRITICISM: SHAKESPEARE, PR 2978.
GRAMMAR: SHAKESPEARE, PR 3075-3081.
HAMLET: FACSIMILES: QUARTOS: SHAKESPEARE, PR 2750.B7.
HAMLET: ORIGINAL EDITIONS: QUARTOS: SHAKESPEARE, PR 2750.A7.
HAMLET: SHAKESPEARE, PR 2807.
HATHAWAY, ANNE: BIOGRAPHY: SHAKESPEARE, PR 2906.
Haunts: BIOGRAPHY: SHAKESPEARE, PR 2915-2920.
HEBREW TRANSLATIONS: SHAKESPEARE, PR 2796.H4.
Henry IV: FACSIMILES: QUARTOS: SHAKESPEARE, PR 2750.B9.
Henry IV: ORIGINAL EDITIONS: QUARTOS: SHAKESPEARE, PR 2750.A9.
Henry IV: SHAKESPEARE, PR 2809.
Henry IV, part 1: FACSIMILES: QUARTOS: SHAKESPEARE, PR 2750.B10.
Henry IV, part 1: ORIGINAL EDITIONS: QUARTOS: SHAKESPEARE,
   PR 2750.A10.
Henry IV, part 1: SHAKESPEARE, PR 2810.
Henry IV, part 2: FACSIMILES: QUARTOS: SHAKESPEARE, PR 2750.B11.
Henry IV, part 2: ORIGINAL EDITIONS: QUARTOS: SHAKESPEARE,
   PR 2750.A11.
Henry IV, part 2: SHAKESPEARE, PR 2811.
Henry V: FACSIMILES: QUARTOS: SHAKESPEARE, PR 2750.B12.
Henry V: ORIGINAL EDITIONS: QUARTOS: SHAKESPEARE, PR 2750.A12.
Henry V: SHAKESPEARE, PR 2812.
Henry VI: FACSIMILES: QUARTOS: SHAKESPEARE, PR 2750.B13.
Henry VI: ORIGINAL EDITIONS: QUARTOS: SHAKESPEARE, PR 2750.A13.
Henry VI: SHAKESPEARE, PR 2813.
Henry VI, part 1: FACSIMILES: QUARTOS: SHAKESPEARE, PR 2750.B14.
Henry VI, part 1: ORIGINAL EDITIONS: QUARTOS: SHAKESPEARE,
   PR 2750.A14.
Henry VI, part 1: SHAKESPEARE, PR 2814.
Henry VI, part 2: FACSIMILES: QUARTOS: SHAKESPEARE, PR 2750.B15.
Henry VI, part 2: ORIGINAL EDITIONS: QUARTOS: SHAKESPEARE,
   PR 2750.A15.
Henry VI, part 2: SHAKESPEARE, PR 2815.
Henry VI, part 3: FACSIMILES: QUARTOS: SHAKESPEARE, PR 2750.B16.
Henry VI, part 3: ORIGINAL EDITIONS: QUARTOS: SHAKESPEARE,
   PR 2750.A16.
Henry VI, part 3: SHAKESPEARE, PR 2816.
Henry VIII: FACSIMILES: QUARTOS: SHAKESPEARE, PR 2750.B17.
Henry VIII: ORIGINAL EDITIONS: QUARTOS: SHAKESPEARE, PR 2750.A17.
Henry VIII: SHAKESPEARE, PR 2817.
HERALDRY: TREATMENT: SHAKESPEARE, PR 3069.H4.

HISTORIES: CRITICISM: SHAKESPEARE, PR 2982.
HISTORIES: SELECTED WORKS: SHAKESPEARE, PR 2762.
HISTORY: TREATMENT: SHAKESPEARE, PR 3014.
HOLINSHED'S CHRONICLES: SOURCES: SHAKESPEARE, PR 2955.H7.
HOMES: BIOGRAPHY: SHAKESPEARE, PR 2915-2920.
Humor: AUTHORSHIP CONTROVERSY: SHAKESPEARE, PR 2948.
Humor: CRITICISM: SHAKESPEARE, PR 2994.
Humor: SOURCES: SHAKESPEARE, PR 2953.W5.
Humour: SELECTIONS: SHAKESPEARE, PR (2773) USE PR 2994.
ICELANDIC TRANSLATIONS: SHAKESPEARE, PR 2789-2790.
ICONOGRAPHY: SHAKESPEARE, PR 2928-2930.
Idealism: CRITICISM: SHAKESPEARE, PR 2986.
IDO TRANSLATIONS: SHAKESPEARE, PR 2800.I2.
ILLUSTRATIONS: SHAKESPEARE, PR 2883.
Imitations: SHAKESPEARE, PR 2877-2879.
Indexes: SHAKESPEARE, PR 2892.
Influence: SHAKESPEARE, PR (2973) USE number for individual author
    influence.
INSANITY: TREATMENT: SHAKESPEARE, PR 3065.
Interpretation: SHAKESPEARE, PR 2965-3088.
IRELAND FORGERIES: MANUSCRIPTS: SHAKESPEARE, PR 2950.
ITALIAN DRAMATIC REPRESENTATIONS: SHAKESPEARE, PR 3109.
ITALIAN SOURCES: SHAKESPEARE, PR 2954.I7.
ITALIAN TRANSLATIONS: SHAKESPEARE, PR 2783-2784.
John: FACSIMILES: QUARTOS: SHAKESPEARE, PR 2750.B18.
John: ORIGINAL EDITIONS: QUARTOS: SHAKESPEARE, PR 2750.A18.
John: SHAKESPEARE, PR 2818.
JONSON: AUTHORSHIP: SHAKESPEARE, PR 2958.J6.
JULIUS CAESAR: FACSIMILES: QUARTOS: SHAKESPEARE, PR 2750.B8.
JULIUS CAESAR: ORIGINAL EDITIONS: QUARTOS: SHAKESPEARE,
    PR 2750.A8.
JULIUS CAESAR: SHAKESPEARE, PR 2808.
KING HENRY IV: FACSIMILES: QUARTOS: SHAKESPEARE, PR 2750.B9.
KING HENRY IV: ORIGINAL EDITIONS: QUARTOS: SHAKESPEARE,
    PR 2750.A9.
KING HENRY IV: SHAKESPEARE, PR 2809.
KING HENRY IV, PART 1: FACSIMILES: QUARTOS: SHAKESPEARE,
    PR 2750.B10.
KING HENRY IV, PART 1: ORIGINAL EDITIONS: QUARTOS: SHAKESPEARE,
    PR 1750.A10.
KING HENRY IV, PART 1: SHAKESPEARE, PR 2810.
KING HENRY IV, PART 2: FACSIMILES: QUARTOS: SHAKESPEARE,
    PR 2750.B11.
KING HENRY IV, PART 2: ORIGINAL EDITIONS: QUARTOS:
    SHAKESPEARE, PR 2750.A11.
KING HENRY IV, PART 2: SHAKESPEARE, PR 2811.

KING HENRY V: FACSIMILES: QUARTOS: SHAKESPEARE, PR 2750.B12.
KING HENRY V: ORIGINAL EDITIONS: QUARTOS: SHAKESPEARE, PR 2750.A12.
KING HENRY V: SHAKESPEARE, PR 2812.
KING HENRY VI: FACSIMILES: QUARTOS: SHAKESPEARE, PR 2750.B13.
KING HENRY VI: ORIGINAL EDITIONS: QUARTOS: SHAKESPEARE, PR 2750.A13.
KING HENRY VI: SHAKESPEARE, PR 2813.
KING HENRY VI, PART 1: FACSIMILES: QUARTOS: SHAKESPEARE, PR 2750.B14.
KING HENRY VI, PART 1: ORIGINAL EDITIONS: QUARTOS: SHAKESPEARE, PR 2750.A14.
KING HENRY VI, PART 1: SHAKESPEARE, PR 2814.
KING HENRY VI, PART 2: FACSIMILES: QUARTOS: SHAKESPEARE, PR 2750.B15.
KING HENRY VI, PART 2: ORIGINAL EDITIONS: QUARTOS: SHAKESPEARE, PR 2750.A15.
KING HENRY VI, PART 2: SHAKESPEARE, PR 2815.
KING HENRY VI, PART 3: FACSIMILES: QUARTOS: SHAKESPEARE, PR 2750.B16.
KING HENRY VI, PART 3: ORIGINAL EDITIONS: QUARTOS: SHAKESPEARE, PR 2750.A16.
KING HENRY VI, PART 3: SHAKESPEARE, PR 2816.
KING HENRY VIII: FACSIMILES: QUARTOS: SHAKESPEARE, PR 2750.B17.
KING HENRY VIII: ORIGINAL EDITIONS: QUARTOS: SHAKESPEARE, PR 2750.A17.
KING HENRY VIII: SHAKESPEARE, PR 2817.
KING JOHN: FACSIMILES: QUARTOS: SHAKESPEARE, PR 2750.B18.
KING JOHN: ORIGINAL EDITIONS: QUARTOS: SHAKESPEARE, PR 2750.A18.
KING JOHN: SHAKESPEARE, PR 2818.
KING LEAR: FACSIMILES: QUARTOS: SHAKESPEARE, PR 2750.B19.
KING LEAR: ORIGINAL EDITIONS: QUARTOS: SHAKESPEARE, PR 2750.A19.
KING LEAR: SHAKESPEARE, PR 2819.
KING RICHARD II: FACSIMILES: QUARTOS: SHAKESPEARE, PR 2750.B20.
KING RICHARD II: ORIGINAL EDITIONS: QUARTOS: SHAKESPEARE, PR 2750.A20.
KING RICHARD II: SHAKESPEARE, PR 2820.
KING RICHARD III: FACSIMILES: QUARTOS: SHAKESPEARE, PR 2750.B21.
KING RICHARD III: ORIGINAL EDITIONS: QUARTOS: SHAKESPEARE, PR 2750.A21.
KING RICHARD III: SHAKESPEARE, PR 2821.
Knowledge of special subjects: SHAKESPEARE, PR 3000-3069.
Laboring classes: TREATMENT: SHAKESPEARE, PR 3021.
LANGUAGE: CRITICISM: SHAKESPEARE, PR (3073)-3088.
LAW: TREATMENT: SHAKESPEARE, PR 3028.

Lear: FACSIMILES: QUARTOS: SHAKESPEARE, PR 2750.B19.
Lear: ORIGINAL EDITIONS: QUARTOS: SHAKESPEARE, PR 2750.A19.
Lear: SHAKESPEARE, PR 2819.
LECTURES: BIOGRAPHY: SHAKESPEARE, PR 2899.
Legal knowledge: SHAKESPEARE, PR 3028.
Linguistics: SHAKESPEARE, PR (3073)-3088.
Literary biography: SHAKESPEARE, PR 2894-2920.
Literature, P.
LITERATURE: TREATMENT: SHAKESPEARE, PR 3037.
LOCRINE: SPURIOUS WORKS: FACSIMILES: QUARTOS: SHAKESPEARE,
    PR 2750.B62.
LOCRINE: SPURIOUS WORKS: ORIGINAL EDITIONS: QUARTOS:
    SHAKESPEARE, PR 2750.A62.
LOCRINE: SPURIOUS WORKS: SHAKESPEARE, PR 2862.
LONDON: BIOGRAPHY: SHAKESPEARE, PR 2907.
LONDON: HOMES: BIOGRAPHY: SHAKESPEARE, PR 2918.
LONDON: MUSEUMS: SHAKESPEARE, PR 2933.L6.
LONDON PRODIGAL: SPURIOUS WORKS: FACSIMILES: QUARTOS:
    SHAKESPEARE, PR 2750.B63.
LONDON PRODIGAL: SPURIOUS WORKS: ORIGINAL EDITIONS: QUARTOS:
    SHAKESPEARE, PR 2750.A63.
LONDON PRODIGAL: SPURIOUS WORKS: SHAKESPEARE, PR 2863.
LOVE: BIOGRAPHY: SHAKESPEARE, PR 2905-2906.
LOVE: TREATMENT: SHAKESPEARE, PR 3069.L6.
LOVER'S COMPLAINT: FACSIMILES: QUARTOS: SHAKESPEARE,
    PR 2750.B49L6.
LOVER'S COMPLAINT: ORIGINAL EDITIONS: QUARTOS: SHAKESPEARE,
    PR 2750.A49L6.
LOVER'S COMPLAINT: SHAKESPEARE, PR 2849.L6.
LOVE'S LABOUR'S LOST: FACSIMILES: QUARTOS: SHAKESPEARE,
    PR 2750.B22.
LOVE'S LABOUR'S LOST: ORIGINAL EDITIONS: QUARTOS: SHAKESPEARE,
    PR 2750.A22.
LOVE'S LABOUR'S LOST: SHAKESPEARE, PR 2822.
LOVE'S LABOUR'S WON: FACSIMILES: QUARTOS: SHAKESPEARE,
    PR 2750.B40.
LOVE'S LABOUR'S WON: ORIGINAL EDITIONS: QUARTOS: SHAKESPEARE,
    PR 2750.A40.
LOVE'S LABOUR'S WON: SHAKESPEARE, PR 2840.
LYLY: SOURCES: SHAKESPEARE, PR 2955.L8.
MACBETH: FACSIMILES: QUARTOS: SHAKESPEARE, PR 2750.B23.
MACBETH: ORIGINAL EDITIONS: QUARTOS: SHAKESPEARE,
    PR 2750.A23.
MACBETH: SHAKESPEARE, PR 2823.
MALE CHARACTERS: CRITICISM: SHAKESPEARE, PR 2992.
MALONE, EDMOND: SCHOLARS: CRITICISM: SHAKESPEARE, PR 2972.M3.

MANUSCRIPTS: SHAKESPEARE, PR 2949-2951.
MARLOWE: AUTHORSHIP: SHAKESPEARE, PR 2958.M3.
Marriage: BIOGRAPHY: SHAKESPEARE, PR 2905-2906.
MATHEMATICS: TREATMENT: SHAKESPEARE, PR 3049.
MEASURE FOR MEASURE: FACSIMILES: QUARTOS: SHAKESPEARE,
    PR 2750.B24.
MEASURE FOR MEASURE: ORIGINAL EDITIONS: QUARTOS: SHAKESPEARE,
    PR 2750.A24.
MEASURE FOR MEASURE: SHAKESPEARE, PR 2824.
MEDICINE: TREATMENT: SHAKESPEARE, PR 3062.
MEMORIALS: SHAKESPEARE, PR 2925-2927.
MERCHANT OF VENICE: FACSIMILES: QUARTOS: SHAKESPEARE,
    PR 2750.B25.
MERCHANT OF VENICE: ORIGINAL EDITIONS: QUARTOS:
    SHAKESPEARE, PR 2750.A25.
MERCHANT OF VENICE: SHAKESPEARE, PR 2825.
MERRY DEVIL OF EDMONTON: SPURIOUS WORKS: FACSIMILES:
    QUARTOS: SHAKESPEARE, PR 2750.B64.
MERRY DEVIL OF EDMONTON: SPURIOUS WORKS: ORIGINAL
    EDITIONS: QUARTOS: SHAKESPEARE, PR 2750.A64.
MERRY DEVIL OF EDMONTON: SPURIOUS WORKS: SHAKESPEARE,
    PR 2864.
MERRY WIVES OF WINDSOR: FACSIMILES: QUARTOS: SHAKESPEARE,
    PR 2750.B26.
MERRY WIVES OF WINDSOR: ORIGINAL EDITIONS: QUARTOS:
    SHAKESPEARE, PR 2750.A26.
MERRY WIVES OF WINDSOR: SHAKESPEARE, PR 2826.
MIDSUMMER NIGHT'S DREAM: FACSIMILES: QUARTOS: SHAKESPEARE,
    PR 2750.B27.
MIDSUMMER NIGHT'S DREAM: ORIGINAL EDITIONS: QUARTOS:
    SHAKESPEARE, PR 2750.A27.
MIDSUMMER NIGHT'S DREAM: SHAKESPEARE, PR 2827.
MONTAIGNE: SOURCES: SHAKESPEARE, PR 2955.M8.
MONUMENTS: SHAKESPEARE, PR 2930.
More, Sir Thomas: SPURIOUS WORKS: FACSIMILES: QUARTOS:
    SHAKESPEARE, PR 2750.B68.
More, Sir Thomas: SPURIOUS WORKS: ORIGINAL EDITIONS: QUARTOS:
    SHAKESPEARE, PR 2750.A68.
More, Sir Thomas: SPURIOUS WORKS: SHAKESPEARE, PR 2868.
MUCEDORUS: SPURIOUS WORKS: FACSIMILES: QUARTOS: SHAKESPEARE,
    PR 2750.B65.
MUCEDORUS: SPURIOUS WORKS: ORIGINAL EDITIONS: QUARTOS:
    SHAKESPEARE, PR 2750.A65.
MUCEDORUS: SPURIOUS WORKS: SHAKESPEARE, PR 2865.
MUCH ADO ABOUT NOTHING: FACSIMILES: QUARTOS: SHAKESPEARE,
    PR 2750.B28.

MUCH ADO ABOUT NOTHING: ORIGINAL EDITIONS: QUARTOS:
SHAKESPEARE, PR 2750.A28.
MUCH ADO ABOUT NOTHING: SHAKESPEARE, PR 2828.
MUSEUMS: SHAKESPEARE, PR 2931-2933.
Music: SHAKESPEARE, PR (2884) *USE* Class M, Music.
Music: TREATMENT: SHAKESPEARE, PR 3034.
MYTHOLOGY: TREATMENT: SHAKESPEARE, PR 3009.
Name: BIOGRAPHY: SHAKESPEARE, PR 2901.
Naturalism: CRITICISM: SHAKESPEARE, PR 2986.
NATURE: TREATMENT: SHAKESPEARE, PR 3039.
Norwegian translations: SHAKESPEARE, PR 2787-2788.
Oceanician translations: SHAKESPEARE, PR 2797.
Oldcastle, Sir John: SPURIOUS WORKS: FACSIMILES: QUARTOS:
SHAKESPEARE, PR 2750.B67.
Oldcastle, Sir John. SPURIOUS WORKS: ORIGINAL EDITIONS:
SHAKESPEARE, PR 2750.A67.
Oldcastle, Sir John: SPURIOUS WORKS: SHAKESPEARE, PR 2867.
ORIGINAL EDITIONS: QUARTOS: SHAKESPEARE, PR 2750.A1-A73.
OTHELLO: FACSIMILES: QUARTOS: SHAKESPEARE, PR 2750.B29.
OTHELLO: ORIGINAL EDITIONS: QUARTOS: SHAKESPEARE, PR 2750.A29.
OTHELLO: SHAKESPEARE, PR 2829.
OUTLINES: ENGLISH COMPREHENSIVE TREATISES: BIOGRAPHY:
SHAKESPEARE, PR 2895.
Outlines: STUDY AND TEACHING: SHAKESPEARE, PR 2987.
OXFORDIAN THEORY: AUTHORSHIP CONTROVERSY: SHAKESPEARE,
PR 2947.
Painting: TREATMENT: SHAKESPEARE, PR 3034.
PAMPHLETS: BACONIAN THEORY: AUTHORSHIP CONTROVERSY:
SHAKESPEARE, PR 2946.
PARAPHRASES: SHAKESPEARE, PR 2877-2879.
PARODIES: SHAKESPEARE, PR 2878.
Partial editions: SHAKESPEARE, PR 2757-2763.
PASSIONATE PILGRIM: FACSIMILES: QUARTOS: SHAKESPEARE,
PR 2750.B47.
PASSIONATE PILGRIM: ORIGINAL EDITIONS: QUARTOS: SHAKESPEARE,
PR 2750.A47.
PASSIONATE PILGRIM: SHAKESPEARE, PR 2847.
PERICLES: FACSIMILES: QUARTOS: SHAKESPEARE, PR 2750.B30.
PERICLES: ORIGINAL EDITIONS: QUARTOS: SHAKESPEARE,
PR 2750.A30.
PERICLES: SHAKESPEARE, PR 2830.
PERIODICALS: BACONIAN THEORY: AUTHORSHIP CONTROVERSY:
SHAKESPEARE, PR 2941.
PERIODICALS: SHAKESPEARE; PR 2885.
PHILOLOGY, P.
PHILOSOPHY: CRITICISM: SHAKESPEARE, PR 2986.

PHILOSOPHY: TREATMENT: SHAKESPEARE, PR 3001.
PHOENIX AND THE TURTLE: SPURIOUS WORKS: FACSIMILES: QUARTOS:
    SHAKESPEARE, PR 2750.B73P47.
PHOENIX AND THE TURTLE: SPURIOUS WORKS: ORIGINAL EDITIONS:
    QUARTOS: SHAKESPEARE, PR 2750.A73P47.
PHOENIX AND THE TURTLE: SPURIOUS WORKS: SHAKESPEARE,
    PR 2873.P47.
PHYSICS: TREATMENT: SHAKESPEARE, PR 3056.
PLOTS: TECHNIQUE: CRITICISM: SHAKESPEARE, PR 2997.P6.
PLUTARCH: SOURCES: SHAKESPEARE, PR 2955.P6.
POEMS: CRITICISM: SHAKESPEARE , PR 2984.
POEMS: FACSIMILES: QUARTOS: SHAKESPEARE, PR 2750.B41-B49.
POEMS: ORIGINAL EDITIONS: QUARTOS: SHAKESPEARE, PR 2750.A41-A49.
Poems: SELECTED WORKS: SHAKESPEARE, PR (2764) *USE* PR 2841-2849.
POEMS: SHAKESPEARE, PR 2841-2849.
POETRY MEMORIALS: SHAKESPEARE, PR 2926.
POLITICS: TREATMENT: SHAKESPEARE, PR 3017.
POLYNESIAN TRANSLATIONS: SHAKESPEARE, PR 2797.
PORTRAITS: SHAKESPEARE, PR 2929.
Portuguese translations: SHAKESPEARE, PR 2793-2794.
Primers: ENGLISH COMPREHENSIVE TREATISES: BIOGRAPHY:
    SHAKESPEARE, PR 2895.
Printing: TREATMENT: SHAKESPEARE, PR 3036.
PRONUNCIATION: SHAKESPEARE, PR 3081.
PROSE: LANGUAGE: SHAKESPEARE, PR 3087.
PROSE MEMORIALS: SHAKESPEARE, PR 2927.
Psychology: TREATMENT: SHAKESPEARE, PR 3001.
PUNS: TECHNIQUE: CRITICISM: SHAKESPEARE, PR 2997.P8.
PURITAN: SPURIOUS WORKS: FACSIMILES: QUARTOS: SHAKESPEARE,
    PR 2750.B66.
PURITAN: SPURIOUS WORKS: ORIGINAL EDITIONS: QUARTOS:
    SHAKESPEARE, PR 2750.A66.
PURITAN: SPURIOUS WORKS: SHAKESPEARE, PR 2866.
QUARTOS: SHAKESPEARE, PR 2750.
Questions: STUDY AND TEACHING: SHAKESPEARE, PR 2987.
Quotations: SHAKESPEARE, PR 2892.
RAPE OF LUCRECE: FACSIMILES: QUARTOS: SHAKESPEARE, PR 2750.B46.
RAPE OF LUCRECE: ORIGINAL EDITIONS: QUARTOS: SHAKESPEARE,
    PR 2750.A46.
RAPE OF LUCRECE: SHAKESPEARE, PR 2846.
Relics: SHAKESPEARE, PR 2931-2933.
RELIGION: TREATMENT: SHAKESPEARE, PR 3011.
Reprints: QUAROTS: SHAKESPEARE, PR 2750.B1-B73.
Richard II: FACSIMILES: QUARTOS: SHAKESPEARE, PR 2750.B20.
Richard II: ORIGINAL EDITIONS: QUARTOS: SHAKESPEARE, PR 2750.A20.
Richard II: SHAKESPEARE, PR 2820.

Richard III: FACSIMILES: QUARTOS: SHAKESPEARE, PR 2750.B21.
Richard III: ORIGINAL EDITIONS: QUARTOS: SHAKESPEARE, PR 2750.A21.
Richard III: SHAKESPEARE, PR 2821.
ROMEO AND JULIET: FACSIMILES: QUARTOS: SHAKESPEARE, PR 2750.B31.
ROMEO AND JULIET: ORIGINAL EDITIONS: QUARTOS: SHAKESPEARE,
    PR 2750.A31.
ROMEO AND JULIET: SHAKESPEARE, PR 2831.
RUSSIAN TRANSLATIONS: SHAKESPEARE, PR 2785-2786.
SATIRE: AUTHORSHIP CONTROVERSY: SHAKESPEARE, PR 2948.
SCANDINAVIAN TRANSLATIONS: SHAKESPEARE, PR 2787-2792.
SCIENCE: TREATMENT: SHAKESPEARE, PR 3047.
SCHOLARS: CRITICISM: SHAKESPEARE, PR 2972.
SECOND FOLIO: SHAKESPEARE, PR 2751.A2.
SELECTED WORKS: SHAKESPEARE, PR 2757-2763.
Selections: Individual works SEE Title of Individual work.
SELECTIONS: POEMS: FACSIMILES: QUARTOS: SHAKESPEARE,
    PR 2750.B42.
SELECTIONS: POEMS: ORIGINAL EDITIONS: QUARTOS: SHAKESPEARE,
    PR 2750.A42.
SELECTIONS: POEMS: SHAKESPEARE, PR 2842.
SELECTIONS: SHAKESPEARE, PR 2767-2771.
SELECTIONS: SPURIOUS WORKS: FACSIMILES: QUARTOS:
    SHAKESPEARE, PR 2750.B52.
SELECTIONS: SPURIOUS WORKS: ORIGINAL EDITIONS: QUARTOS:
    SHAKESPEARE, PR 2750.A52.
SELECTIONS: SPURIOUS WORKS: SHAKESPEARE, PR 2852.
SHAKESPEARE, PR 2750-3112.
Shakespeare apocrypha, PR 2851-2875.
Shakespeare apocrypha: FACSIMILES: QUARTOS: PR 2750.B51-B73.
Shakespeare apocrypha: ORIGINAL EDITIONS: QUARTOS, PR 2750.A51-A73.
Shakespeare-Bacon controversy, PR 2941-2948.
Shakespeare jest books, PR 2953.W5.
SHAKESPEARIAN THEORY: AUTHORSHIP CONTROVERSY: SHAKESPEARE,
    PR 2939.
Signatures: SHAKESPEARE, PR 2949-2951.
SIR JOHN OLDCASTLE: SPURIOUS WORKS: FACSIMILES: QUARTOS:
    SHAKESPEARE, PR 2750.B67.
SIR JOHN OLDCASTLE: SPURIOUS WORKS: ORIGINAL EDITIONS:
    QUARTOS: SHAKESPEARE, PR 2750.A67.
SIR JOHN OLDCASTLE: SPURIOUS WORKS: SHAKESPEARE, PR 2867.
SIR THOMAS MORE: SPURIOUS WORKS: FACSIMILES: QUARTOS:
    SHAKESPEARE, PR 2750.B68.
SIR THOMAS MORE: SPURIOUS WORKS: ORIGINAL EDITIONS: QUARTOS:
    SHAKESPEARE, PR 2750.A68.
SIR THOMAS MORE: SPURIOUS WORKS: SHAKESPEARE, PR 2868.
SLAVIC TRANSLATIONS: SHAKESPEARE, PR 2795.

Societies: BACONIAN THEORY: AUTHORSHIP CONTROVERSY:
   SHAKESPEARE, PR 2941.
SOCIETIES: SHAKESPEARE, PR 2887-2889.
SOCIOLOGY: TREATMENT: SHAKESPEARE, PR 3024.
SOLOLOQUIES: TECHNIQUE: CRITICISM: SHAKESPEARE, PR 2997.S7.
SONNETS: FACSIMILES: QUARTOS: SHAKESPEARE, PR 2750.B48.
SONNETS: ORIGINAL EDITIONS: QUARTOS: SHAKESPEARE, PR 2750.A48.
SONNETS: SHAKESPEARE, PR 2848.
SOURCES: SHAKESPEARE, PR 2952-2955.
SPANISH SOURCES: SHAKESPEARE, PR 2954.S7.
SPANISH TRANSLATIONS: SHAKESPEARE, PR 2793-2794.
SPORTS: TREATMENT: SHAKESPEARE, PR 3067.
SPURIOUS WORKS: FACSIMILES: QUARTOS: SHAKESPEARE,
   PR 2750.B51-B73.
SPURIOUS WORKS: ORIGINAL EDITIONS: QUARTOS: SHAKESPEARE,
   PR 2750.A51-A73.
SPURIOUS WORKS: SHAKESPEARE, PR 2851-2875.
STRATFORD: BIOGRAPHY: SHAKESPEARE, PR 2908.
STRATFORD: HOMES: BIOGRAPHY: SHAKESPEARE, PR 2916.
STRATFORD: MUSEUMS: SHAKESPEARE, PR 2932.
STUDY AND TEACHING: SHAKESPEARE, PR 2987.
Style: CRITICISM: SHAKESPEARE, PR (3073)-3088.
THE SUPERNATURAL: TREATMENT: SHAKESPEARE, PR 3004.
SUSPENSE: TECHNIQUE: CRITICISM: SHAKESPEARE, PR 2997.S8.
SWEDISH TRANSLATIONS: SHAKESPEARE, PR 2791-2792.
Syllabi: STUDY AND TEACHING: SHAKESPEARE, PR 2987.
Snyopses: STUDY AND TEACHING: SHAKESPEARE, PR 2987.
SYNTAX: SHAKESPEARE, PR 3078.
TAMING OF THE SHREW: FACSIMILES: QUARTOS: SHAKESPEARE,
   PR 2750.B32.
TAMING OF THE SHREW: ORIGINAL EDITIONS: QUARTOS: SHAKESPEARE,
   PR 2750.A32.
TAMING OF THE SHREW: SHAKESPEARE, PR 2832.
Teaching and study: SHAKESPEARE, PR 2987.
Technical arts: TREATMENT: SHAKESPEARE, PR 3036.
TECHNIQUE: CRITICISM: SHAKESPEARE, PR 2995-2997.
TEMPEST: FACSIMILES: QUARTOS: SHAKESPEARE, PR 2750.B33.
TEMPEST: ORIGINAL EDITIONS: QUARTOS: SHAKESPEARE,
   PR 2750.A33.
TEMPEST: SHAKESPEARE, PR 2833.
Testimonials: SHAKESPEARE, PR 2925-2927.
Textual commentaries: SHAKESPEARE, PR 3070-3071.
TEXTUAL CRITICISM: SHAKESPEARE, PR 3070-3071.
Textual emendations: SHAKESPEARE, PR 3070-3071.
THEATERS: LONDON: BIOGRAPHY: SHAKESPEARE, PR 2920.
Theatrical presentations: SHAKESPEARE, PR 3091-3112.

THIRD FOLIO: SHAKESPEARE, PR 2751.A3.
THOMAS, LORD CROMWELL: SPURIOUS WORKS: FACSIMILES: QUARTOS:
SHAKESPEARE, PR 2750.B69.
THOMAS, LORD CROMWELL: SPURIOUS WORKS: ORIGINAL EDITIONS:
QUARTOS: SHAKESPEARE, PR 2750.A69.
THOMAS, LORD CROMWELL: SPURIOUS WORKS: SHAKESPEARE, PR 2869.
Thoughts: SELECTIONS: SHAKESPEARE, PR 2770-2771.
TIME RELATIONS: TECHNIQUE: CRITICISM: SHAKESPEARE, PR 2997.T5.
TIMON OF ATHENS: FACSIMILES: QUARTOS: SHAKESPEARE, PR 2750.B34.
TIMON OF ATHENS: ORIGINAL EDITIONS: QUARTOS: SHAKESPEARE,
PR 2750.A34.
TIMON OF ATHENS: SHAKESPEARE, PR 2834.
TITUS ANDRONICUS: FACSIMILES: QUARTOS: SHAKESPEARE,
PR 2750.B35.
TITUS ANDRONICUS: ORIGINAL EDITIONS: QUARTOS: SHAKESPEARE,
PR 2750.A35.
TITUS ANDRONICUS: SHAKESPEARE, PR 2835.
TRAGEDIES: CRITICISM: SHAKESPEARE, PR 2983.
TRAGEDIES: SELECTED WORKS: SHAKESPEARE, PR 2763.
TRANSLATIONS: SHAKESPEARE, PR 2775-2800.
TRANSLATIONS: SHAKESPEARE, PR 2881.
TREATMENT: SHAKESPEARE, PR 3000-3069.
Treatment of life: CRITICISM: SHAKESPEARE, PR 2989-2993.
TREATISES: BIOGRAPHY: SHAKESPEARE, PR 2894-2920.
TREATISES: CRITICISM: SHAKESPEARE, PR 2975-2979.
TROLUS AND CRESSIDA: FACSIMILES: QUARTOS: SHAKESPEARE,
PR 2750.B36.
TROLUS AND CRESSIDA: ORIGINAL EDITIONS: QUARTOS: SHAKESPEARE,
PR 2750.A36.
TROLUS AND CRESSIDA: SHAKESPEARE, PR 2836.
TWELFTH NIGHT: FACSIMILES: QUARTOS: SHAKESPEARE, PR 2750.B37.
TWELFTH NIGHT: ORIGINAL EDITIONS: QUARTOS: SHAKESPEARE,
PR 2750.A37.
TWELFTH NIGHT: SHAKESPEARE, PR 2837.
TWO GENTLEMEN OF VERONA: FACSIMILES: QUARTOS: SHAKESPEARE,
PR 2750.B38.
TWO GENTLEMEN OF VERONA: ORIGINAL EDITIONS: QUARTOS:
SHAKESPEARE, PR 2750.A38.
TWO GENTLEMEN OF VERONA: SHAKESPEARE, PR 2838.
TWO NOBLE KINSMEN: SPURIOUS WORKS: FACSIMILES: QUARTOS:
SHAKESPEARE, PR 2750.B70.
TWO NOBLE KINSMEN: SPURIOUS WORKS: ORIGINAL EDITIONS:
QUARTOS: SHAKESPEARE, PR 2750.A70.
TWO NOBLE KINSMEN: SPURIOUS WORKS: SHAKESPEARE, PR 2870.
UNITIES: TECHNIQUE: CRITICISM: SHAKESPEARE, PR 2997.U5.
USE OF WORDS: SHAKESPEARE, PR 3077.

VENUS AND ADONIS: FACSIMILES: QUARTOS: SHAKESPEARE,
   PR 2750.B45.
VENUS AND ADONIS: ORIGINAL EDITIONS: QUARTOS: SHAKESPEARE,
   PR 2750.A45.
VENUS AND ADONIS: SHAKESPEARE, PR 2845.
VERSIFICATION: SHAKESPEARE, PR 3085.
VOLAPUK TRANSLATIONS: SHAKESPEARE, PR 2800.V8.
VORTIGERN: SPURIOUS WORKS: FACSIMILES: QUARTOS: SHAKESPEARE,
   PR 2750.B71.
VORTIGERN: SPURIOUS WORKS: ORIGINAL EDITIONS: QUARTOS:
   SHAKESPEARE, PR 2750.A71.
VORTIGERN: SPURIOUS WORKS: SHAKESPEARE, PR 2871.
Warwickshire: HOMES: BIOGRAPHY: SHAKESPEARE, PR 2916.
Will: BIOGRAPHY: SHAKESPEARE, PR 2908.
WINTER'S TALE: FACSIMILES: QUARTOS: SHAKESPEARE, PR 2750.B39.
WINTER'S TALE: ORIGINAL EDITIONS: QUARTOS: SHAKESPEARE,
   PR 2750.A39.
WINTER'S TALE: SHAKESPEARE, PR 2839.
WIT: CRITICISM: SHAKESPEARE, PR 2994.
Wit: SELECTIONS: SHAKESPEARE, PR (2773) *USE* PR 2994.
WIT: SOURCES: SHAKESPEARE, PR 2953.W5.
Women: BIOGRAPHY: SHAKESPEARE, PR 2905-2906.
Women: CHARACTERS: CRITICISM: SHAKESPEARE, PR 2991.
Writing; SHAKESPEARE, PR 2949-2951.
YIDDISH TRANSLATIONS: SHAKESPEARE, PR 2800.Y5.
YORKSHIRE TRAGEDY: SPURIOUS WORKS: FACSIMILES: QUARTOS:
   SHAKESPEARE, PR 2750.B72.
YORKSHIRE TRAGEDY: SPURIOUS WORKS: ORIGINAL EDITIONS:
   QUARTOS: SHAKESPEARE, PR 2750.A72.
YORKSHIRE TRAGEDY: SPURIOUS WORKS: SHAKESPEARE, PR 2872.
YOUTH: BIOGRAPHY: SHAKESPEARE, PR 2903.
ZOOLOGY: TREATMENT: SHAKESPEARE, PR 3044.

SHAKESPEARE FEATURE CARDS
CLASSIFIED ARRAY

English renaissance (1500-1640),
   PR 2199-3195.
Individual authors, PR 2417-3195.
Separate works, PR 2750.A1-A40.
Special poems, PR 2750.A43.
Separate works, PR 2750.B1-B40.
Special poems, PR 2750.B43.

Other poems, PR 2750.A49.
Special works, PR 2750.A54-A73.
Special works, PR 2750.B54-B73.
Others, by title, A-Z, PR 2750.A73A-Z.
Others, by title, A-Z, PR 2750.B73A-Z.
18th century, by editor, A-Z,
   PR 2752.A-Z.

19th century, by editor, A-Z,
   PR 2753.A-Z.
20th century, by editor, A-Z,
   PR 2754.A-Z.
General, PR 2757-2759.
Early, to 1800, PR 2757.
Recent, PR 2759.
To 1800, PR 2767.
1801- , PR 2769.
To 1800, PR 2770.
1801- , PR 2771.
Separate works, A-Z, PR 2776.A-Z.
Early (to 1800), PR 2777.
Recent, PR 2778.
Separate works, A-Z, PR 2779.A-Z.
Early (to 1800), PR 2780.
Recent, PR 2781.
Separate works, A-Z, PR 2782.A-Z.
Separate works, A-Z, PR 2784.A-Z.
Separate works, A-Z, PR 2786.A-Z.
Separate works, A-Z, PR 2788.A-Z.
Separate works, A-Z, PR 2790.A-Z.
Separate works, A-Z, PR 2792.A-Z.
Separate works, A-Z, PR 2794.A-Z.
Other European. By language A-Z,
   PR 2795.A-Z.
Other languages, PR 2796-2800.
Separate works, PR 2801-2840.
Special poems, PR 2843.
Other poems, PR 2849.
Special works, PR 2854-2873.
Others, by title, A-Z, PR 2873.A-Z.
Special works (including parodies),
   by title, A-Z, PR 2878.A-Z.
Other, PR 2879.
Other, PR 2889.
Other, A-Z, PR 2898.A-Z.
Other, PR 2913.
General works, history, etc., PR 2928.
Other, by place, A-Z, PR 2933.A-Z.
General, PR 2937.
Early (to 1800), PR 2943.
Recent, PR 2944-2945.
Other, PR 2945.
Other hypotheses, A-Z, PR 2947.
General works, PR 2952.

Special. By subject, A-Z, PR 2953.A-Z.
Special authors or works, A-Z, PR
   2955.A-Z.
General, PR 2957.
Special, A-Z, PR 2958.A-Z.
History of Shakespearian criticism,
   PR 2965-(2973).
General, PR 2965.
By period, PR 2967-2969.
17th century, PR 2967.
18th century, PR 2968.
19th century and later, PR 2969.
By country, A-Z, PR 2971.A-Z.
Early, to 1800, PR 2975.
Recent, PR 2976.
Other, PR 2979.
Special forms, PR 2981-2984.
General, PR 2989.
Special, PR 2991-2993.
Groups. Classes, PR 2991-2992.
Other, A-Z, PR 2992.A-Z.
Individual, PR 2993.
General works, PR 2995.
Special, by subject, A-Z, PR 2997.
General works, PR 3000.
Other special subjects, A-Z, PR
   3069.A-Z.
Early works, PR 3070.
Recent, PR 3071.
General, PR 3075.
Special, PR 3077-3081.
Other, A-Z, PR 3081.A-Z.
General, PR 3091-3092.
Other, PR 3092.
By period, PR 3095-3099.
Elizabethan, PR 3095.
17th-18th centuries, PR 3097.
19th-20th centuries, PR 3099.
Separate plays, with text, PR 3105-
   3109.
By country, PR 3105-3109.
Other, PR 3109.